Railways In Preservation

Isle Of Wight R
40 years of preservation

Dave Walker & Terry Hastings

Nostalgia Road Publications

CONTENTS

The **Nostalgia Road** Series ™

is produced under licence by

Nostalgia Road Publications Ltd.

Units 5 - 8, Chancel Place, Shap Road Industrial Estate,

Kendal, Cumbria, LA9 6NZ

Tel. +44 (0)1539 738832 - Fax: +44 (0)1539 730075

designed and published by

Trans-Pennine Publishing Ltd.

PO Box 10, Appleby-in-Westmorland, Cumbria, CA16 6FA

Tel. +44 (0)17683 51053 Fax. +44 (0)17683 53558

e-mail: admin@transpenninepublishing.co.uk

and printed by

Kent Valley Colour Printers Ltd.

Kendal, Cumbria - +44 (0)1539 741344

Front Cover: *Isle of Wight Steam Railway flagship locomotive W24* Calbourne *storms past milepost 3¹/2 with a down train for Wootton.* **IWR Collection**

Rear Cover Top: *W24* Calbourne *looks resplendent after overhaul complete with smaller bunker, poses in the up loop at Havenstreet.* **IWR Collection**

Rear Cover Bottom: *Here, typifying the island services, 8* Freshwater *passes through Ashey.* **IWR Collection**

Title Page: *Newly out-shopped in BR black, Newport poses at Smallbrook on a special charter.* **IWR Collection/ R.Pelham**

This Page: *Classic shot of Havenstreet station with both of our A1X class terriers.* **IWR Collection**

FOREWORD

I was very touched when asked to write the foreword to this most informative book on the Isle of Wight Steam Railway, because I had something to do with its formation all those many years ago.

Memories tend to fade but I seem to remember it all started with my reading about the Westerham Locomotive Preservation Society when I met David Perry. He was a little boy in those days and so was I, and we were all slightly crazy. However, we were part of a group of railway enthusiasts, rapidly increasing in number all over the nation. Without really realising what we were doing, we were determined in a gathering momentum of feverish activity to save something of our steam age that was dying out, not in a blaze of glory but in the degradation of dirt and

Above: *The focus of preservation efforts in 1967, W24 Calbourne, shown here as restored with original short bunker, at Ashey Station in 1993.* IWR Collection

grime. In 1967, it seemed that authority was determined to even scrap almost new steam engines to move prematurely into the shining new age of diesel and electrics.

I was feverishly trying to record on canvas some feeling of those days and I was also caught by the preservation bug! I was surrounded by my friends selling Biro pens and calendars to buy a Merchant Navy Pacific, whilst others sent in £50 deposits for a Duchess Pacific, but I think that BR deserved the greatest credit because they were trying to run a railway while all this was going on!

CORRESPONDENCE.

"To the Editor, Southern Railway Magazine.
An appeal from an old engine, Isle of Wight. (1928)

In my old age I make this appeal to you. Can you do anything to avoid me meeting the usual fate of old engines? I shall have been in service 50 years in March, so I am anxious regarding my final end. My big brother Gladstone has been preserved, cannot something be done for me? I'm only a little chap and should not take up much room. There is an old railway coach standing at Waterloo, it is not in the way and is a source of interest to many. How attractive I should look - say at London Bridge - restored to my original livery, name and number and the record again placed on my tanks that I won a gold medal at the Paris Exhibition in 1878. I could still be useful if a box was attached for contributions to the Railway Orphanage. Was it not owing to my prowess that the journey between London and Paris was considerably quickened? Did I not show the Frenchmen what speed was and how to do it? Surely I am worth a better fate than to be scrapped. Hoping, sir, you will be able to set the ball rolling for my preservation and thus earn the appreciation of a large section of the general public and the everlasting gratitude of your humble servant. 'W' 11".

Top Left: *Towyn, 30th July 1964. A snatched picture of 32640 formerly (W11 Newport) on its Flatrol in a 'pick-up goods' train en-*route *for Pwllheli and its first period of preservation.* David J. Mitchell

Middle Left: *The* Southern Railway Magazine, *and the letter that started it all.*

Bottom Right: *W13 Ryde awaiting preservation.* A.B. MacLeod IWR Collection

I remember going to Ian Allan's office in Shepperton to ask for some advice and they gave it to me; "David, if you have £500 to spend, why don't you buy an 02 Class tank engine?" I didn't know what he was talking about, but *Calbourne* soon became ours and I have such happy memories of visiting the Isle of Wight on the very last days of steam and, at the same time, doing a quick sketch of Ryde St John's shed from life. So it was *Calbourne* that started it all for me, even before the fateful telephone call which led me to purchase *Black Prince* and the *Green Knight*, but that is another story.

Doctor Beeching certainly did his work, as we all know. We so often say, "If only!" Surely, on the Isle of Wight at that time, there was a strong case for preserving the whole line and the entire infrastructure. The Island had a fleet of beautiful little tank engines and gorgeous old railway coaches, so what happened?

Bureaucracy destroyed almost all of it, and replaced it with ancient London underground coaches, which didn't even fit the station platforms! However, let us look at what has since been achieved. What the Isle of Wight preservationists have saved is now a major tourist attraction, unique in having preserved down to the finest detail, the feeling of a Victorian railway. Nevertheless, I now believe that in these increasingly hard times, when we are faced with more and more bureaucracy and regulation, the Isle of Wight Steam Railway can meet the challenge with confidence. I believe that in the next ten years the preservation scene will change out of all recognition, but the steam railway will still be running on the Isle of Wight, giving an increasing number of tourists who hunger for the past, a feeling of an age when events and things happened just a little more slowly. The railway will also be introducing people to quality and a touch of romance, and what's wrong with that?

Good luck!

David Shepherd

David Shepherd OBE, FRSA, FRCS

EARLY PRESERVATION – SOME YOU WIN ....!

This is the story of a unique railway, and covers a 40-year history of standard gauge railway preservation on the Isle of Wight. The Island had never seen a modern railway, and even when line closures came in the 1950s and '60s, the British Railway services were operated by small tank locomotives and an eclectic collection of rolling stock. If those railways could have been preserved in aspic, they would have looked and represented Victorian and Edwardian railways at their best. The rural lines that connected the beauty spots, seaside resorts and ferry terminals were at one time the Island's lifeblood, and the holidaymaker's delight, but their truly seasonal peaks and troughs made them mostly uneconomic from the outset. Yet when they were placed under threat from the 1950s onwards, a terrific campaign to stop closure was mounted. Successful in parts, and completely in vain in the long run, only the section from Ryde to Shanklin would escape closure when it was electrified and operated with antiquated tube train stock discarded by London Underground.

The demise of steam operation in 1966 was generally regarded as the start of the preservation era in the Isle of Wight. Fortunately this was not quite the case, for both by accident and design some vehicles from the earlier period managed to survive. As far back as February 1928 an appeal appeared in the *Southern Railway Magazine*. Whilst this heart-felt plea may not have produced an immediate response, W11 ultimately saw a new life in preservation after selection by Butlin's for display at Pwllheli holiday camp in 1964.

Not so lucky was W13 *Ryde* a Beyer-Peacock 2-4-0T of 1864, which had been built for the original Isle of Wight Railway. Withdrawn in 1932 after 1.5 million miles service, the engine was rescued by Alistair MacLeod, Commercial Manager and Divisional Operating Superintendent for the Southern Railway on the Island. *Ryde* was cosmetically restored and turned out in photographic grey in a style approximating the old IW Railway livery. On 13th June 1934, *Ryde* made its final trip via the floating crane to Southampton and on to Eastleigh for storage. Tragically a World War II scrap drive finally led to W13's destruction! This was particularly sad, as history now reveals that the fervent reclamation of metals, of which the Southern Railway contributed no less than 255,379-tons, was to have been largely a morale-boosting propaganda move, from which the main beneficiaries were scrap merchants.

The Ryde Pier Tramway was opened in 1864, and in 1871 the Ryde Pier Company ordered a single-deck tramcar, which was ultimately to become No.4. It was also named the 'Grapes' car, as it had its external corner posts elaborately carved with ornate grapes; work done by one H. S. Jones of Newport. Soon after delivery a top deck was added, only to have this removed in 1886 when the railway was electrified. On 6th September 1935 the 'Grapes' car was pushed through the buffer stops at Ryde Pier Head and was considered to be beyond economical repair. The remains were acquired by Mr H. Winstone, the body work restored, and the resultant rebuild donated to the Hull Transport Museum, in whose care it has been ever since. These attempts were not a particularly auspicious start to Island railway preservation, but they were certainly indicative of the random way in which exhibits were to be rescued and their later restoration prioritised.

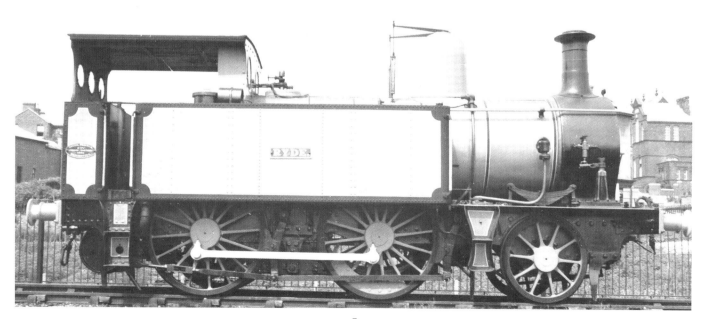

FOUNDING FATHERS

Above: *The Sadler Rail Coach in the down platform at Droxford 24th September 1967*. Richard J. Newman

It is safe to say that the current preservation scene in the Isle of Wight owes its existence to two people, Ron Strutt and David Perry. Both had a passion unsurpassed and a drive that would ultimately see their paths take very different courses. In the early 1960s, the 12-year-old Ron wrote to BR offering to purchase W14 *Fishbourne* for a deposit of £5 and then pay a 1/- (5p) a week thereafter - needless to say this was refused. In the summer of 1965, shortly before one of the closure dates proposed for the Island railways, Ron visited the system as part of a Duke of Edinburgh Silver Award Scheme. Through the good offices of the Public Relations Department at Waterloo and local assistance from inspector Ron Russell, Ron Strutt and friend Iain Whitlam had free range of the system; box visits, goods train rides - the lot! This was the magic spark that lit the fire of passion. Having learned that closure of the Cowes-Ryde line had been deferred to February 1966 and that only the Ventnor- Shanklin section was to go the following April, it was decided that a chance existed to rescue something of the old steam railway.

At a meeting called in October 1965, various interested parties including two respected railway professionals attended. One of these was Alan Blackburn, who initially regarded the whole thing as a hopeless case, but thankfully later went on to Chair the Isle of Wight Railway Company. Also attending was David Perry - a person very much involved with the stillborn Westerham Railway Museum. David had very different ideas about preservation, but he had the drive and know-how to move things forward. The initial concept was to take over the Cowes-Ryde line in association with the IW Council, but negotiations were somewhat protracted; no doubt justifiably fuelled by scepticism. In the meantime the Vectis Electric Railway (Vectrail) put forward proposals for overhead electrification of the soon to be closed sections. Their proposals were remarkably similar to those for the Hayling Island branch some three years previously, and in this form was soon to meet the same fate!

The use of internal combustion railcars was a far more suitable option, and a sponsor in the form of Charles Ashby of Sadler Railcoach fame, came to the fore.

In April the Wight Locomotive Society (WLS) was founded and it set a target of £1,500 to purchase an O2 Class locomotive and carriages. The stock was offered at £900 for the engine and £52 for each coach. A press and promotional campaign raised the grand sum of £32! Ron Strutt later wrote, "youth has a number of advantages; one is the inability to recognise a hopeless cause." The matter was not helped by a proliferation of schemes all intent on saving locomotives and stock from the Island. Things looked bleak for the nascent WLS and only the timely intervention of artist David Shepherd and a donation of £500 saved the day. Ron Strutt went on to note, "David's role in the Society has often been hinted at, but few people will be aware just how important a part he played. His support both in its generosity and its timing, changed our prospects overnight", and what is more there was "no doubt whatsoever, that had it not been for David Shepherd, there would be no Isle of Wight Railway today."

In November 1966 the WLS team together with David Shepherd visited the Island to select 'their' engine. Meetings also took place at Ryde to form an Island committee to oversee day-to-day matters; preparations were made for the last day of steam on 31st December 1966. Last day philatelic covers and collecting boxes raised over £100, whilst contributions from such worthies as Sir Peter Allen were very much welcomed. David Shepherd and the team made the best of the occasion and left Shanklin by steam for the last time on the delayed 10.12pm to Ryde St John's Road. In the event various other plans to purchase O2 Class locomotives came to naught and No.24 *Calbourne*- originally reserved for a local tourist attraction, became available and was ultimately selected for preservation by the Wight Locomotive Society.

Top Right: *W28* Ashey *storms out of Cowes Station on a very damp 13th February 1966. The grimy weather does not improve the poor condition of the locomotives, but this is perhaps understandable as the line is just a week away from the withdrawal of passenger services. Freight would last longer, but only until 16th May 1966.* Terry Hastings

Middle Right: *David Shepherd about to board W24* Calbourne *for a ride back to the depot on 7th November 1966. On this visit W22* Brading *was selected for preservation, however the later availability of W24, which at the time was destined to be stuffed and mounted at Calbourne Mill, saw Brading consigned to the breaker's yard along with the remaining O2 Class engines.* Iain Whitlam

Bottom Right: *David Shepherd watches anxiously as a wreath is placed on the bunker of W14* Fishbourne *during the evening of 31st December 1966 to mark the 'Farewell To IOW Steam'.* Terry Hastings

WEEP NOT FOR WHAT IS GONE

The latter half of 1966 was a time for new arrivals. In preparation for electrification 12 single bolsters, converted from Lowfit wagons, were transferred together with the Matisa tamper DS72. At Eastleigh a Hunslet Class 05 diesel (D2554) was readied for the Island, upon arrival this locomotive was the most modern piece of equipment on the system and was promptly christened *Nuclear Fred*. In the Spring of 1967, there soon followed two ex-Southern Railway 15-ton goods brake vans. Subsequently all the above, with the exception of four bolster wagons, were to find their way to the Isle of Wight Steam Railway.

By the end of steam, a dozen ex-London & South Western Railway (LSWR) 02 Class locomotives remained on the Island. Of these W18 *Ningwood* had been cannibalised at Ryde, and its remains were towed to Newport on 22nd December 1966; the following month it was moved down to the Cement Mills siding, where it was broken up by H. B. Jolliffe of Somerton.

A further nine locomotives were hauled to Newport and stored in the bay platform, thus leaving W24 *Calbourne* and W31 *Chale* at Ryde on engineering duties. On 18th April 1967, W27 *Merstone* became the last Island locomotive to be steamed by British Railways when it was used to shunt its condemned sisters from Newport station into the nearby Freshwater yard; for its pains it was the first to succumb to the cutter's torch! The locomotives scrapped by H. B. Jolliffe of Somerton, were as follows:

No.	Name	Date Scrapped
W27	*Merstone*	April 1967
W16	*Ventnor*	May 1967
W20	*Shanklin*	May 1967
W35	*Freshwater*	May/June 1967
W28	*Ashey*	June 1967
W17	*Seaview*	June/July 1967
W33	*Bembridge*	July 1967
W14	*Fishbourne*	July 1967
W22	*Brading*	July/Aug 1967

Top Left: *Newly arrived, the Matisa Tamper DS72 is seen in the dock road at Brading in December 1966.* Terry Hastings

Middle Left: *Awaiting their fate in March 1967, at Newport. Condemned locomotives went with a touch of dignity as a gang had recently given them a quick wipe down with an oily rag.* Terry Hastings

Bottom Left: *On 18th April 1967,* Merstone *performs its last duty for BR, shunting condemned stock at Newport.* Iain Whitlam

Top Right: *D2554 complete with* Nuclear Fred *nameplate at Ryde St. Johns' Road in early 1968.* Terry Hastings

Middle Right: *Another 02 Class ends its days in a pile of scrap and asbestos in July 1967.* Peter Ford

Bottom Right: *Although they look ready for work, this is the first batch of condemned carriages, which are captured in their storage area in the Freshwater Yard at Newport in May 1966 before the cutting commenced.* Terry Hastings

By March 1967 W24 and W31 were withdrawn, whilst *Calbourne* was offered for sale on 2nd May 1967; amazingly it entered preservation just 20 days later. Meanwhile, *Chale* remained at Ryde and work commenced on cutting in September. A brief respite was afforded by the breaker's yard (A. King & Son of Norwich), whilst eleventh-hour preservation attempts came from the mainland. Sadly this was not to be and the locomotive's remains were carted by road to Newport, to join the scrap mountain accumulated from broken coaching stock. Of the rolling stock, about 20 carriages were condemned in early 1966 with the closure of the Cowes line; they too were taken to Newport and broken up by Jolliffe's.

The end of the summer service saw around 30 vehicles sold to King's of Norwich, included in this batch was SECR composite saloon 6375; fortunately this was rescued by the Wight Locomotive Society. King's also bought about 60 wagons in November and a further 29 came to Newport in December.

The eleven remaining carriages, ten wagons and four ex-LSWR 'road' vans arrived for breaking in January 1967. Amongst the withdrawn vehicles were two ex-London, Brighton & South Coast Railway (LBSCR) Brake Second coaches (4156/65), which were reserved for the Bluebell Railway; whilst the Kent & East Sussex Railway hoped to acquire the ex-South Eastern & Chatham (SECR) Second 2453. However, it appears that prohibitive transportation costs dashed these proposals, and this was also the main reason why the eleventh-hour attempt to save *Chale* also failed.

Fortunately all was not lost; SECR brake 4149 was purchased privately and was destined for transportation to Canada! However circumstances changed and the carriage was eventually acquired by a donation to the WLS. In addition the following coaches were also saved; LBSCR Third 2416, LBSCR Brake Third 4168, LBSCR Composite 6349 and SECR Brake Third 4145. All the rescued coaching stock was marshalled into the platforms at Newport, but then the real headaches began! Fortunately the days of the graffiti artist were yet to come, but mindless destructive vandalism, which is now so prevalent, was about to start. The acts of 'souvenir' hunters and possible accidental damage was also of great concern. Security was difficult and many brass fittings were removed in a pre-emptive attempt to prevent theft. In addition nightly patrols were the norm and it was not uncommon for members to spend days-on-end living in the stock especially over school holidays and weekends.

Top Left: *Pass the super-glue please! Newport's Freshwater Yard on 23rd June 1967.* Richard J. Newman

Middle Left: *Set alight by the scrapmen in the Freshwater yard, the old carriages burn fiercely.* R. Silsbury collection

Bottom Left & Right: *This vehicle (LSWR Van 548) had been reserved for preservation but vandals are no respecters of history. Here we see it first on 7th January 1967, and after the damage on 20th March 1967.* Richard J. Newman

Although regarded as somewhat extreme at the time, one can only point out that today, almost 40-years on, these vehicles still exist and most are in regular traffic! Regretfully, LSWR van No.548 was not so lucky as it was set alight by vandals in March 1967. Later that month the scrap merchants decided to torch the wooden-bodied carriages as they were taking too long to break - their charred remains littered the yard at Newport until November when the metal work was recovered.

Although purchased for preservation, back at Ryde, W24 was also subjected to theft as its temporary painted nameplates and various brass fittings were removed by persons unknown and never seen again - or so we thought. Amazingly during the summer of 2006 a gentleman presented the Steam Railway's General Manager with a display panel on which were bolted many of the missing items-but alas not the nameplates! The old Isle of Wight Railway crane 425S was moved from the Island in the summer of 1967 and secured a place in preservation with its original manufacturers, Kirkstall Forge Ltd. Other historic items also left the Island, initially bound for the Transport Museum at Clapham but these would eventually come under the wing of the National Railway Museum at York. These were; LSWR Road van No.56055, LBSCR Cattle wagon No.53374, LSWR Car truck No.60562, SR Coal wagon No.27884. All four of these wagons were stored at Fratton for sometime before heading off to Preston Park (Brighton) on the 18th November.

A New Day Dawns

On 20th March 1967 a service of electric trains commenced operating on the Island's truncated railways between Ryde Pier Head and Shanklin. To do this a fleet of 43 ex-London Transport 'Standard' tube cars were employed. Modified electrically and refurbished, they were formed into twelve sets, six three car (3TIS) and six four car (4VEC). These vehicles and a replacement for one accident damaged car remained in service, albeit with a steady withdrawal programme until 1992, by which time they had been superseded by 18 much more modern(?) 1938 motor cars.

None of the 'standard' stock was preserved on the Island although it was offered but five vehicles were returned to LT in October 1990 for inclusion in a heritage set. These were S2S, S7S, S27S, S44S and S49S. Ryde Works undertook the repainting of S27S and S44S into early Underground liveries before dispatch. Back at Newport in 1967 work progressed on carriage restoration although most of the effort was put into preventing deterioration due to weather and rot.

Sunday 26th January 1969 saw the closure of the Ryde Pier tramway. With enough on its plate already, the Wight Locomotive Society felt unable to launch a rescue plan but a small splinter group known as the Island Vintage Transport Group made the effort. Collections were arranged and leaflets distributed; and a jolly good time was had by all! After the event, the Treasurer was able to report that enough had been raised to purchase Car No.2 and the resultant funds were safely secured in his Post Office savings account! It was not until a year later that the car was 'dismantled' and the chassis moved to Newport. It later went on to play a vital part in the establishment of the Steam Railway at Havenstreet, but unfortunately by 1972 it was set aside and like so many things in preservation it still awaits its restoration to this very day!

Two important stock purchases in 1969 were LBSCR road vehicle truck No.60579 and LSWR road van No.56046. Both were at Ryde, together with three LBSCR bolsters and two SR coal wagons, which were reserved for Vectrail. On 26th July British Road Services moved all seven vehicles to Newport with labour supplied by the Wight Locomotive Society.

Top Right: *At first sight, an unremarkable picture of Crompton diesel D6541 at Havant on 18th November 1967. However, the view records what was probably the fastest and longest journey for the ex-IW vehicles for more than 40 years! The LSWR Road Van, LBSCR Cattle Wagon, LSWR Cartruck and SR coal wagon are making their last main line trip from Fratton to Preston Park, Brighton, before joining the national collection.* Richard J. Newman

Bottom Right: *A new day dawns. This poster pictured at Brading station proclaims the coming of the 'New' (ex-LT tube stock) service between Ryde and Shanklin from 20th March 1967. This started after a 3 month closure of the line to facilitate electrification work.* Terry Hastings

BRITISH RAILWAYS

NEW!
Isle of Wight electric train service from 20th. March

RYDE · BRADING · SANDOWN · SHANKLIN with connecting bus service to Wroxall and Ventnor

For details ask for folder

British Rail Southern Region

Top Left: *In November 1966, awaiting its next turn of crew training along the Portsmouth direct route, a former London Underground 4-VEC set (No.043) is seen at Fratton.*
Terry Hastings Collection

Middle Left: *At Ryde Works in 1990, cars S27S and S44S (right) await return to the mainland having been respectively re-painted in 1920s and '30s style. Sadly cars S2S, S7S and S44S are currently under threat from the cutters torch and are stored in the open at Acton Works.* Ray Maxfield

Bottom Left: *The very last tram from Ryde Pier Head on Sunday 26th January 1967. Left to right are Fred Ward, Hughie White (driver), Des Hawkins, Marion Hunnisett and Tom Cadman.*
Terry Hastings

The unloading of the lighter trucks was performed by the 100-year-old ex-Midland Railway crane, but the larger items awaited the heavy lift machine. Rail crane 429S and its match truck 429SM had previously been acquired by Vectrail and were housed at Newport awaiting their anticipated take over of the Ryde-Cowes railway. Ultimately the Steam Railway secured both for preservation in 1971.

Meanwhile back at Ryde, the severing of the Cowes line connection at Smallbrook had effectively stranded *Calbourne* at St. John's Road and various methods of removal were investigated. Some bizarre proposals came up, ranging from an army exercise to the joint purchase of a low-loader with the Tramway Museum Society (who wanted to move a tram from Prague to Crich). In the event the chance arrival of a suitable low-loader on the Island on 11th August prompted this writer to contact the haulage company. The detailed account of the next few days is a book in itself, however *Calbourne* left Ryde on Friday 15th August 1969 and was unloaded in the Freshwater yard, Newport the following day.

At last, all the preserved stock was in one place and all that was needed was to make it operable, as Tommy Cooper might have said "Just like that." Behind the scenes all was not too rosy. Rental for the stock storage at Newport was crippling and most of the hard-earned funds went in that direction. Hand-over of the track bed from BR to the IW Council was taking its time and there appeared to be little progress on the Vectrail front. In the event, the WLS decided a fall-back plan was needed and so it prepared its own case to acquire a section of line on which to house and operate its preserved stock. This proposal was spearheaded by Des Hawkins, Richard Newman, George Wheeler and this author. The ultimate failure of the Vectrail plan in the autumn of 1970 was more a matter of relief than sadness, for it meant the 'preservationists' could come out from behind the curtain and take their rightful place in negotiating the future for the Island's railway heritage.

On behalf of the Wight Locomotive Society, George Wheeler attended an interesting and what may well be a unique site meeting with the British Rail Board representative and various invited scrap merchants who were bidding for the Ryde to Cowes railway track.

Above: *Lots of activity at Ryde on Saturday 26th July 1969, as George Wheeler and Terry Hastings wrestle with a wayward LSWR van. To the right was one of our greatest disappointments, DS70008, former Brighton-built invalid saloon as it awaits breaking. All we could save from it were a few droplights, a set of springs and the only on-board toilet to run in the Island since the 1930s.*
Iain Whitlam

Above: *Here, ex-Midland Railway crane 429S unloads a Vectrail wagon in the Freshwater yard at Newport on 26th July 1969.*
Iain Whitlam

Below: *Calbourne is on a Wynns' AEC low loader as it rounds the corner 'wrong road' at Ryde's Parish Church on 15th August 1969; this was one of the biggest loads hauled by road on the Island at this time.* Richard J. Newman

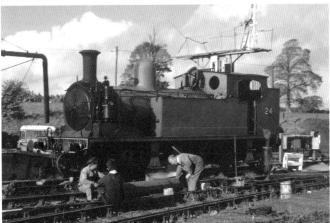

Top Left: *Lots of familiar faces are pushing baby home on 17th August 1969. With the help of Peter Peel's tractor, eager volunteers manhandle No.24 from its delivery point in Newport's Freshwater Yard round to the station.* Richard J. Newman

Middle Left: *Here 02 Class No.24* Calbourne *is being 'passed out' by the boiler inspector in the autumn of 1970.* Terry Hastings

Bottom Left: Calbourne *and train appear to head off for Cowes on 8th November 1970, but it is only a test run at the limit of our operation in Newport.* Terry Hastings

A deal was struck whereby the scrapmen would each put forward two bids; one for the whole line and a second bid that excluded the one-mile 50-chains of track at Havenstreet, a length of plain line at Newport and sundry other items such as water tanks, buffer stops, pointwork etc. wanted by the WLS. At a subsequent meeting at the London offices of the BRB Supplies & Contract Manager, David Perry successfully got the BRB to let the WLS pay the difference on the accepted bid, without extras or penalties. It was a tremendous relief to all that such favourable terms were agreed. The IW Council in its turn agreed a favourable lease on the track bed from Wootton to Smallbrook Junction thus the right of way was protected for any future extension.

With the help of Bob Huxtable, Tom Jackman and team, *Calbourne* passed its hydraulic test in the Spring of 1970 and after lengthy negotiations with our landlords, it was allowed to carry out testing operations around Newport within station limits. The first public appearance was on 8th November when a train of bogie stock headed off for Cowes, or at least as far as the Newport Home Signal! Negotiations to purchase the Wootton-Havenstreet section and a lease on the trackbed were underway. Gangs led by Mike and Alan Brittan set to work on the track between Newport and Havenstreet as replacement keys (borrowed from the Cowes-Newport section) were transported on the old Ryde Pier tram. It was known that time at Newport was running out, so everything had to be made ready to move. With the best will in the world no one could think that the WLS was ready when notice to quit arrived on 20th January 1971 - all had to be gone by Monday the 25th!

A further volume would be needed to cover the events of those five days alone, but history shows the job was done. By 8.30pm on 24th January the very last train left Newport followed by Ryde Pier tramcar No.2 some 20-minutes later. As an aside to this event, one of the last trains through Whippingham station stopped to pick up a letter addressed to Her Majesty The Queen. Whippingham had been the local station for Osborne House, residence of Queen Victoria. The letter was further conveyed to Buckingham Palace, by Alderman Mark Woodnutt who was then the Island's MP. A reply dated 27th January 1971 from the Queen's Private Secretary expressed Her Majesty's interest and best wishes. Not bad for the railway's first day; but little did anyone realise this was to be followed by a series of Royal visits spanning the next 30-years, all of which proves that it pays to advertise!

Top Right: *November 1970, a gang starts clearance on the track at Fairlee (near Newport) en-route to Havenstreet. Close examination of the picture gives an indication of the mammoth task involved, The almost pristine track in the foreground disappears into complete greenery just beyond the trolley. Not only did four years of mother nature's work need to be cleared, but many of the wooden keys holding the rails in the chairs had been removed by people to burn on open fires being cheaper than logs or coal! The missing keys needed replacing with steel ones "borrowed" from the Newport-Cowes section to make the line safe for the imminent move out to a new home at Havenstreet.* Terry Hastings

Middle Right: *Ready for the 'off' on 24th January 1971. The water supply to the tower had been terminated about a week before. In desperation, the track drains were blocked and the resultant 'flood' pumped into water tanks and the locomotive. Ryde Pier tram No.2 stands on the right.* Terry Hastings

Bottom Right: *The Wight Locomotive Society ran six trips from Newport to Havenstreet clearing its rolling stock and other worldly goods on 24th January 1971. The first and last runs were operated by the former Ryde Pier tram No 2: the remaining four were hauled by 02 Calbourne. In this view, the tram sets off with the first trip of the day loaded with water barrels; 'Hyviz' Hastings drives, whilst hanging on grimly is John Wenyon. Alan Brittan is seated by the engine with string and sealing wax in case of failure!*
John Woodhams

Below: *Whippingham station on 24th January 1971. Alderman Mark Woodnutt (left) and Bob Huxtable. The bag contains a letter to HM The Queen, advising her of the last train through the Royal Station.* Richard J Newman

ISLE OF WIGHT STEAM RAILWAY - A SLOW BIRTH

Above: *The first day for the Isle of Wight Steam Railway. W24 Calbourne at the head (or rear?) of a train. Services were push/pull worked for some years. This view marks the very early days of operations, being taken on 12th April 1971, and might be interestingly compared with others later in this book.* Richard J. Newman

Taking stock at Havenstreet was frightening; one locomotive, six bogie coaches, a few old wagons, plus one and five-eighths miles of derelict single line, a small station building, one island platform and very little else. Except perhaps about 90-tons of steam coal, acquired by Tom Jackman. Unfortunately transport from the mainland, by rail twice and road three times had taken its toll! The resultant material was little more than dust, which just fitted into Tom's five-inch gauge locomotives perfectly; we suspected his motives. However this fuel supply saw the embryonic steam line through the first 18-months; all for about £100!

Frantic activity was required to enable the first public trains to operate on Easter Monday, when W24 operated a push-pull service with three bogie coaches between Havenstreet and Woodhouse crossing - about a mile down the line. Almost 1,000 people turned out and as a result, interest in the scheme grew rapidly. New members and offers of help were welcomed, especially as the existing team were stretched to the limit. In the background and over time, deals were struck for track and land and a limited liability company, The Isle of Wight Railway Company (hereafter referred to simply as the Railway), was set up to operate the line. It was clear from the start that the provision of workshop facilities and further motive power were a priority.

During May of 1971 Southampton businessman Tom Jefferis was standing outside this writer's office with a quantity of ex-Southern Vectis buses, which he was about to ship back to the mainland. A flippant remark to Tom enquiring if he had any railway engines provoked an amazing reply; he had about eight of them, most ex-military narrow gauge diesels and one 0-4-0ST *Invincible*, which had run on the standard gauge Royal Aircraft Establishment railway at Farnborough. What was more, Tom was looking for a home for it, so on 3rd June *Invincible* arrived on free loan; and was first steamed on 28th December, the day after *Calbourne's* 80th birthday.

Whilst all this was taking place, the National Motor Museum at Beaulieu was disbanding its Bournemouth Belle exhibit. The Schools Class locomotive *Stowe* was off to pastures new and the caretaker Beaulieu Pullman Group were looking for a home for two of the three Pullman cars left on site. Here was an opportunity for on-train catering in opulent surroundings, the like of which had never before been seen on the Island.

Top Right: *Some of Tom Jackman's coal arrives at Havenstreet in 1971 the remainder had come earlier, in one of the last trains that had made the journey by rail from Newport in 1971.*
Terry Hastings

Middle Right: *The first steam engine to use a car ferry to reach the Isle of Wight,* Invincible *is seen here boarding the MV* Fishbourne *at Portsmouth on 3rd June 1971.* Terry Hastings

Bottom Right: Invincible *takes a dive! An interesting, if not rather unconventional way to unload a locomotive was captured on film at Havenstreet on 3rd June 1971.* Terry Hastings

Whilst these were not local vehicles, the marketing and commercial potential was too good to miss. Consequently, *Agatha* and *Fingall* arrived in April/May 1972. Unfortunately after initial enthusiasm, the two members of the BP Group waned in their interest and both cars were left in a semi-derelict state for some years. Eventually their ownership was transferred to the Steam Railway and *Agatha* left the Island for Carnforth in September 1977. Initially *Fingall* was retained but an offer from the Bluebell Railway saw its departure in June 1979 for a far more fitting life in preservation.

The shortage of motive power was still a problem in 1972 but with the timely offer of a diesel and a further steam locomotive it was hoped would save the day. The Ruston & Hornsby locomotive *Spitfire* arrived on 6th June, whilst 0-6-0T *Ajax* (a 1918-built Andrew Barclay) followed on 30th November. The diesel saw intermittent service on the Island until 1988, after which its owner transferred it to the Northamptonshire Ironstone Railway Trust. On the other hand, *Ajax* was to become the railway's Cinderella, overshadowed and overtaken by events.

In July 1972 two ex-LBSCR coal wagons 28345/27766 were added to the fleet. There were also the first rumblings that negotiations with Butlin's were going well and Terrier W11 *Newport* may be on its way home. These were being carried out on the railway's behalf by Sir Peter Allen, who was a keen supporter of the Island's railways, and as a young graduate had penned the first definitive history of its railways. Published in 1928, *The Railways of the Isle of Wight* went on to become a collector's item. Peter had also become life-long friends with A. B. MacLeod, the Southern Railway's man on the Island and one suspects that he may have 'assisted' the letter from 'W11' that we mentioned earlier.

Sir Peter's negotiations in 1972 were successful, and on 27th January 1973 *Newport* was loaded aboard the car ferry MV *Fishbourne*. During the crossing, the WLS entertained their special guests, including Sir Peter Allen, A. B. MacLeod, David Shepherd, C. Hamilton Ellis and Geoffrey Kitchenside to name but a few of the considerable names in the realms of railway history and preservation. Sir Peter was always one to put his money where his mouth was and as a result he insisted that W11 should be restored, at least cosmetically, to IWCR livery complete with Wheeler & Hurst chimney.

Top Left: *Pullman cars* Agatha *and* Fingall *make a sad sight at Beaulieu in March 1972. The Beaulieu Pullman Group had already disposed of a Third Class car and was looking to the Isle of Wight for a long-term home for the remaining vehicles.* Terry Hastings

Middle Left: Agatha *makes an undignified arrival at Havenstreet in April 1972.* Terry Hastings

Bottom Left: *Ruston & Hornsby* Spitfire *is craned onto the track in June 1972.* Terry Hastings

Bottom Right: *Haulage contractors, Pointers had used the wrong tractor unit when taking* Ajax *to the island as it exceeded the weight limit on the ferry deck. So Wight Locomotive Society members and ferry staff at Fishbourne, located a suitable tractor on a rig and a 'whip round' found sufficient funds to allow the driver of the Dawson Freight Volvo to help out. Here, the tractor is about to couple-up at Portsmouth. The ferry company employed one of the authors at the time and he had been able to arrange for this trans-shipment, but he was severely reprimanded by the Divisional Manager for this service delay and its attendant problems!* Terry Hastings

To this end the engine was delivered to Ryde works where some of this work was to be carried out. However, it was not until two years later that No.11 with little signs of progress, was taken to Havenstreet to have the job completed. For sometime the railway's trains had been operated on a push-pull system, an electric bell connected the trailer 'cab' to the locomotive and an emergency brake handle were all that was considered necessary. Under this arrangement, the locomotive was always marshalled on the downhill (Havenstreet) end and trains terminated either in the old coal siding or on the main line adjacent Station Road bridge at Wootton. After an engineering survey it was decided that it would be possible to stabilise a slippage in the cutting that had once formed Wootton station that closed back in 1953.

Work began on excavation and drainage, with the intention of forming a six-car platform with run round on the Whippingham side where the track bed opened out. All went well with this splendid plan until the end of 1973, when heavy rain caused another major slippage. The teams wrestled with the problems for some months, but the final straw came in the winter of 1974 when a lorry delivering coal to the Station House found the driveway disappearing. The work was abandoned and the cutting filled in to stabilise the situation.

In September 1973 the railway was offered a LCDR Brake Third No.4115 that lay at Atherfield, still in full Southern malachite livery. It was almost two years later, after a 25-year accumulation of chicken guano had been removed, that the body found its way to Havenstreet. Back in the yard at Havenstreet, Alan Blackburn and his assistants constructed a locomotive servicing pit, whilst a further siding was laid off to the south and plans were made for the construction of workshop facilities.

Top Right: *Railway members David Perry, George Wheeler and Nick Robinson went up to Butlin's at Pwllheli at the end of 1972 to oil up the engine. Unfortunately, numerous stones that had been pushed down the chimney and fallen into the cylinders escaped attention, and this proved an expensive mistake!* Terry Hastings

Middle Right: *Sir Peter Allen (right) and A.B. MacLeod admire Newport's fine lines at Fishbourne on 27th January 1973!* Terry Hastings

Bottom Right: *During the autumn of 1971 Ray Maxfield dug a small inspection pit outside the signal box at Havenstreet. The digger was at tea when this picture was taken.* Terry Hastings

Below: *The ill-fated effort to save the original Wootton station sees Dave Nye, Nick Robinson and Kevin Moon labour in vain to put things right.* John Goss

RYDE - NEWPORT
100 YEARS NOT-OUT

Above: *Impudence or what? The diminutive W37 takes Pullman car Agatha for a 'spin' to test clearances. April 1972.* Terry Hastings

The year 1975 was not only remarkable for the celebrations of the Ryde-Newport centenary, but also a near record year for accumulating old junk or historic vehicles, depending on your point of view. An eight-ton Isle of Wight Central Railway (IWCR) van body (No.86) arrived in May, followed by the redundant tamper DS72 in June along with IWR Composite coach No.38 that came from Hayling in July. A further IWR vehicle No.39 was also on offer, whilst a selection of eight-plank wagons were obtained from Medina Wharf.

To date, parts from the eight-planks have been reused in a restored look-alike, the tamper broken for scrap whilst others await their turn for restoration. Happier is the story of a North London Railway coach of 1864. It came to the Island in 1898 as IWR No.46 but was withdrawn sometime in the late 1920s, the body was then removed to Hayling Island and converted into a bungalow. It too was secured in 1975 and restoration started in 1981. It is currently in service on the Steam Railway as SR No.6336.

In August 1975 the steam railway celebrated with a daily train service and a three-day extravaganza of vintage road vehicles. On 24th August, Alistair MacLeod and Sir Peter Allen unveiled the restored No.11 and congratulated Chris Whiting who, in addition to overseeing the job was also responsible for the execution of award winning publicity artwork for the line. Nearly 300 people braved the elements on 20th December to celebrate the real centenary and the local TV station featured the line during its regional news programme.

A matter of days later Sir Peter Allen was on the phone to advise that His Excellency the Governor of the Island, Earl Mountbatten of Burma wanted to visit! Panic overdrive ensued but all was ready for the 50-minute visit on the 22nd January. The usual introductions made, His Excellency insisted on riding in the cab of No.24 and promptly took charge of the locomotive; 'clearly he had done it before', said driver Ray Maxfield who, along with fireman Len Pullinger, now IW Railway Chief Mechanical Engineer, just let him get on with it!

During this period, the infrastructure of the Steam Railway remained a matter of concern; workshop construction was underway, albeit slowly, but the abandonment at Wootton of the western terminus plan led to the burning of much midnight oil. The new scheme for a single platform, run round loop and siding east of the Station Road Bridge met with approval.

In preparation the railway acquired a quantity of trackwork from Bedhampton Waterworks, near Havant, and with its own labour lifted, sorted and transported it to Havenstreet ready for re-use. The crossing keeper's hut from Smithards Lane, Cowes, was temporarily placed over the Wootton ground-frame, later to be replaced by the former Freshwater Signal box. The hut then moved to Havenstreet and served as a Booking Office until the end of 2004 and is now used as a car park attendant's shelter on special events.

The yard at Havenstreet had been in a bit of a pickle for some time, having housed sundry items such as water towers, tanks, concrete sleepers, locomotive boilers, buffer stops etc., so a concerted effort was needed to have a grand clear up. Quantities of paling fencing were acquired from Woolston and Droxford and installed around the site. The yard area was then levelled with ash and the whole site took on a look of respectability. Further arrivals in 1976 included PMV No.1052 from Ryde works as an ex-stores van, along with the sheerlegs. Sadly this latter item, which took some considerable dismantling, was destined never to be re-erected.

Although not apparent at the time, important events were taking place elsewhere with the rescue of a further item from the Ryde Pier Tramway; an old 1871 Starbuck horse tram. This had then been turned into the 'first' electric motor car on the pier, but it had been withdrawn in 1927 before seeing further life as a holiday chalet in Brighstone. During 1978 it was rescued privately for preservation and after a peripatetic couple of years, the body was finally restored in the mid-1980s. After a period at the erstwhile Cothey Bottom Heritage Centre, Ryde, it went on to become a star exhibit at the Isle of Wight Bus Museum at Newport on 5th March 2000.

Back at the station, electric lighting was installed in the building for the first time and all hands stood by to receive Wickham trolley DS3320, which (after some accident damage) was declared redundant at Sandown and purchased for further use on the Steam Railway.

Area supporters groups once played an important part in the line's development. For example, in the Midlands, Andrew Britton and Frank Hodges raised funds for a new ballast box for the old Midland Railway crane. Most funding came from sales and talks, one of the most interesting being on the 'Railways of the Island of Sodor' by the Reverend Wilbert Awdry!

Top Right: *The look-alike eight-plank coal wagon resplendent in SR livery.* Dave Walker

Middle Right: Invincible *sets off in the rain to celebrate the start of Centenary Week in August 1975.* Terry Hastings

Bottom Right: *Chris Whiting in grey suit waits the unveiling of No.11 at the Centenary Show of 1975.* Terry Hastings

Top Left: *Lord Louis Mountbatten at Havenstreet on his visit. Pictured are (left to right) the late-Paul Gomes, Alan Blackburn, Roger Silsbury, Lord Louis and Kim Chalkley.* Peter J. Relf

Middle Left: *Restored Pier Tramcar leaving the Cothey Bottom Heritage Centre for the IW Bus Museum on 5th March 2000. Derek Hunt and Dave Greenwood Senior & Junior lend a hand.* Richard J. Newman

Bottom Left: *Another coup was a steam railtour from Leamington Spa to Tyseley and back, hauled by* Clun Castle *on 3rd April 1978. Here, the GWR locomotive arrives for servicing at Tyseley on the Midland Wightman's railtour.* Terry Hastings

Below: *The Signal & Telegraph (S&T) Department under the leadership of George Wheeler was particularly active in the summer of 1976, rescuing the Up Home bracket signal from Sandown and re-siting it to the down end of Havenstreet platform. It was again relocated in 2000 to become the Havenstreet Down Inner Home. The S&T team also acquired a six-lever ground-frame and another LSWR lower quadrant signal post complete with fittings. The much-travelled bracket signal is seen below in its new position when pictured in September 2002 after a fresh coat of paint.* Dave Walker

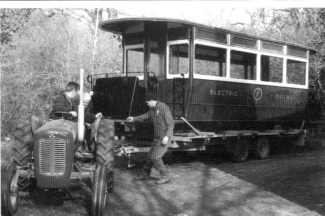

DEALS FOR WHEELS

Towards the end of 1977, the first ever National Exhibition of Railway Art was also run by the Midland Group. Over 21 respected artists showed 151 works at the Railart Event. Opened by David Shepherd on 4th November, more than 3,000 visitors filed through the display. However, the proceeds from this particular event were destined for the World Wildlife Fund.

Work progressed steadily at Wootton on the new station site and on 21st August 1977, No.W24 *Calbourne* ran round a train here for the first time although the platform was yet to be completed. Further arrivals included part of LCDR 2418 an IWR blue top-light coach of 1864 and IWR four-compartment Second No.39, ex-Hayling Island.

In January 1978, *Calbourne* took its old LSWR number of 209 when the BBC arrived in force to film John Alderton in an episode of Wodehouse Playhouse called *The Smile That Wins*. Somehow Havenstreet became Charing Cross at night and on re-viewing a tape recently available, it really did look quite good! The abilities developed by the Isle of Wight Steam Railway were beginning to pay dividends, and a deal with the National Railway Museum saw the railway lift a SER turnout during an engineers' occupation near Merstham in exchange for the loan of the LBSCR cattle wagon. The vehicle returned to the Island on 21st March 1978.

Above: *Isle of Wight Steam Railway staff working on the 'mainline' lifting a SER turnout at Merstham for the* National Railway Museum. Iain Whitlam

Relations further benefited by the presentation of an original *Newport* nameplate to David Perry by Dr. John Scholes, Keeper of the National Collection. This was to be included along with the original *Calbourne* plate in the museum, which at that time was housed in the Fairview cottage next to Havenstreet station. Yet more ex-Sandown engineers' stock was acquired for £380 and on 15th May six wagons DB450157, 451289, 451924, 452018, 452715 and 453374 arrived.

Sir Peter Allen had been hard at work with brewers Whitbread who owned W8 *Freshwater*, which had been stuffed and mounted in its original guise as *Newington,* outside the *Hayling Billy* public house. Many parties were reputed to be in negotiations for this engine, but in the end it was sold for a nominal sum to the Steam Railway. Chris Whiting completely re-painted the engine at Hayling in two weekends so that when it was moved on 18th June, it was truly an Isle of Wight loco; complete with SR lining and *Freshwater* nameplates. Shortly after the hand-over on 9th August, Engineering Officer Len Pullinger wrote; "Generally the locomotive is in excellent condition, and shows little sign of having stood on a plinth for 13-years, one-month and one-day with a boiler full of water and a firebox full of clinker!"

Top Left: *David Perry (left) receives the* Newport *nameplate from Dr. John Scholes at the NRM York.* British Rail, Eastern Region

Middle Left: *W8* Freshwater *is found outside the* Hayling Billy *public house very shortly before its removal to Havenstreet. In addition to painting the engine, Chris Whiting also made the GRP replica nameplates.* Roger Silsbury

Bottom Left: *Here W8* Freshwater *is pictured with (left to right) A. B. MacLeod, Tony Bray (Freshwater Council), Sir Peter Allen, Roger Silsbury (Chairman IWR Co. Ltd), George Sumner (Chairman Whitbread Wessex Ltd).* IWSR Archive/R. C. Riley

Further arrivals came that summer with DS62888, a four-plank truck of 1899, built for the Great Central construction and later sold to the SER in 1901, which arrived on 5th July. Two other vehicles from Sandown were also disposed of at this time, one went to the Bluebell, the other to Swanage. They were 4 plank dropsides which in 1966/7 had been converted to Engineers wagons from 7 or 8 plank coal wagons. One was DS 27744 which eventually returned to the Island.

On the 7th June, W8 was also on the move, as it went by low-loader to Yarmouth to celebrate the 150th Anniversary of the Lymington-Yarmouth ferry route; interestingly this was the first of this engine's many excursions away from the railway. In September 1980, W8 moved under its own power for the first time since May 1966 and was joined on the railway by a North British diesel shunter that had come from Esso's refinery at Fawley. Although still incomplete, the new workshop at Havenstreet received its first project on 3rd January 1981, when the frames of W11 were ceremonially pushed inside. Also to benefit was W8, as the new works gave the final 'tweaks' enabling the engine to enter traffic on the 27th June. On 3rd October, the body of LCDR five-compartment Third Class coach No.2515 arrived, another vehicle I am pleased to report is now back in regular traffic.

This is perhaps a suitable point to spare a thought for the Permanent Way team who, in addition to looking after the track, also have a rather large garden to maintain. The Isle of Wight Steam Railway, in 1981, had about three and a half miles of fencing to look after on the main line to Wootton and a further six and a half miles on the unused section to Smallbrook. About 75% of this had been re-fenced by the Southern Railway or later by British Railways, but the rest clearly remained in a decayed IW Central condition; and one suspects that one or two remote sections may have even gone back to the days of the Ryde & Newport Railway!

To restore it we had to first find the section of fence, but this was usually buried under years of undergrowth and saplings all of which not only had to be cleared but disposed of. Lengths of up to a quarter of a mile were tackled at a time and in 1980 a serious start was made to bring the lineside fencing up to scratch.

At this stage it may be appropriate to say a brief word or two about what may appear to be the Railway's indiscriminate collections policy with regard to rolling stock! With respect to coaching stock, we actively collect bodies of ex-Island vehicles or identical mainland examples if the originals exist; of these the best examples are saved whilst the others are broken up to provide parts. The same is true with wagons, but in addition more modern vehicles are retained for Engineers' duties, thus releasing historical items to restoration. The running gear for both categories are provided by donors, so batches of vehicles are acquired for no apparent historical reason; some of these may be further used, broken up for spares, or sold on to other groups.

That said another 11 vehicles arrived in 1982, these were: S1566 PMV, S1750 CCT and S1783 PMV, plus DB450665 and DB451341 (both Single Bolsters), and Open Ballast trucks DB483700, DB483701, DB483725 and DB483733. In addition, two tank cars were donated by Esso, these being 1231 of 1916 and 1343 of 1918. These were reputed to be similar to the Royal Daylight tank cars that once ran on the Island. Incidentally, for the modellers, a '00' (4mm) scale model of 1343 was available from Bachmann Europe plc in 2003/04.

Around about this time a number of government schemes were promising opportunities for youngsters and adults alike to learn new skills, so the Steam Railway was not slow in 'sponsoring' projects like Youth Opportunities Programmes. Amongst these schemes was a new refreshment building at Havenstreet, which was designed in-house by Chris Whiting to accommodate a museum and café. It was opened with due ceremony on Saturday 18th September 1982 by Bernard Kaukas Dip.Arch (hons). RIBA. M.Inst. ENV, Sc.FRSA. Director (Environment) for the British Railways Board.

Part of the unused track-bed between Rowlands Lane and Ashey was turned into a conditional bridle-way but with specific safeguards to allow its re-use as a railway. At the time, the track-bed between Havenstreet and Smallbrook was leased from the IW Council to protect the railway's right of way.

Top Right: *The North British diesel named* Tiger *is seen on a rare passenger working at Wootton.* Terry Hastings

Middle Right: *A forgotten moment during 1980 was the centenary of the opening of the railway pier at Ryde on 12th July 1880. Here, the headboard supplied by George Wheeler was carried on the pier shuttle service all day.* Terry Hastings

Bottom Right: *Loosely quoting from Mrs. Beeton's famous cookery and recipe book, this picture might be captioned 'First find your fence', but as can be seen, this could be a little difficult. This is a 2002 project with trackman Peter Corby literally getting to grips with nature.* Dave Walker

1983 - This Was Not A Good Year!

Challenge 1983 made a big splash, its aim was to raise £90,000 for three key projects; a new museum and shop, the restoration of W11, and the restoration of four-wheeled carriages. The idea was for a new layout for visitor's facilities at Havenstreet (the first of many), which included a splendid purpose-built museum and shop to be constructed by a gang on another Government-sponsored labour team, but watch this space!

In December 1982 considerable excitement followed the acquisition of crane runner DS3107 (an ex-LSWR carriage underframe), which was just the right donor for LCDR bogie Brake Third No.4115. All looked ready for the line's first bogie restoration project and removal of the underframe from Eastleigh scheduled for 18th March. However, on 7th March contractors cut up the attached crane and the match truck, even though BR Staff on site tried to prevent this. The Steam Railway's Chairman, Roger Silsbury, described the action as "an act of sheer vandalism!" who could fail to agree?

For some years our eyes had been focused on the former gasworks retort house at Havenstreet, which was then used as a barn. The building had a delightful Victorian industrial design and would convert well into modern use for the expanding Steam Railway, so the building, together with another nearby was acquired.

Above: *The IWR's re-creation of a small Island terminus at Wootton, incorporates the 19th century ticket collector's hut from Ryde Pier Head. In this image, the quaint nature of a 'Victorian' country station can be clearly seen.* IWR Collection

Further acquisitions were also made, including a quantity of real estate adjacent to the station. It has to be said that in subsequent years considerable land purchases have been made around the station, and these have proved particularly fortuitous with regard to storage of all the miscellany that inevitably goes with preserved railways.

Wagon DB450665 was converted into a boiler washout truck, with the addition of a water tank and pump during 1983 and was re-numbered 665S. Soon after, further wagon work was carried out by pupils of Bembridge School under the leadership of Alan Doe including, and as part of the Duke of Edinburgh Award Scheme they refurbished drop-side wagon No.62888 and returned it to Southern Railway livery. Meanwhile, the museum curator was particularly excited by the arrival of a collection of name and builder's plates from the old IWR's Beyer-Peacock locomotives. These were donated on loan from the private collection of Sir Peter Allen, and were soon joined by a collection from Alistair MacLeod, which included a plate from the ill-fated W13 *Ryde*.

Top Right: *The new café/museum building was a huge step forward in our catering facilities, but it subsequently lost the museum section to make more room and has been extended twice!* IWR Collection

Centre Right: *Some of the newly acquired open ballast wagons being taken for an 'airing' behind* Vectis, *which in fact was* Invincible *during the brief period when it was re-named after the Island's bus company instead of a famous World War I battle cruiser! Whilst on the subject,* Ajax *is also named after a Royal Navy battleship of 1913 vintage, and not a Dutch football team as one onlooker recently suggested!* Terry Hastings

Bottom Right: *The pupils of Bembridge School restored this drop-side wagon, No.62888, in SR livery.* IWR Collection

These nameplates continue to be an important exhibit to this day. A four-plank drop-side DS27744 that had earlier escaped the Island for Purbeck, returned on 12th November that year and was reported as suitable for 'spares'. Unfortunately an ex-LSWR composite coach body at Chale was not so lucky and due to its inaccessibility could not be saved.

The Signal & Telegraph gangs were hard at work in Wootton, where we had an entirely new station with interesting connections. As part of the commitment to retention of historical items, the S&T work at Wootton was a good example: The lever frame was part of that from Shanklin, the signal box was of FYN origins at Newport station, whilst the lattice signal posts came from Netley (Up Starter) and St. Denys (Down Branch Starter). Signage from Netley joined the ticket collector's hut from Ryde Pier to help create the right atmosphere.

April 1984 saw the arrival of a British Railways Class 03 (03079) at Ryde to replace *Nuclear Fred* (97803), which was acquired by the IW Steam Railway for static display. However, its gearbox problems were not quite as bad as feared and the engine has remained operating on light duties ever since. Two further PMVs were acquired in 1985, 1046 and 1048 together with a 15-ton SR goods brake van No.55710. The PMV's were destined as donor underframes, whilst the van was intended to support the ageing LSWR road van No.56046 already in preservation.

Meanwhile, IWR Composite No.46 was nearing completion and saw daylight on 20th January; externally it looked wonderful and was only waiting for the trimmers to complete the upholstery. Further additions to the working engineers' fleet included ex-LT ballast hoppers HW437 and 435 and a 20-ton Lowmac No.DS61056. The Lowmac was re-decked immediately and the two hoppers later turned out in Southern Railway style and renumbered 63437 and 63435 respectively.

The sales shop, which had for some years been located in the Waiting Room at Havenstreet was finally relocated to a new structure adjacent to the gas retort house. Sales Manager Nick Boycott had overseen the fitting out and was ready to start trading from his new base at Christmas.

The work was completed by Easter 1986 and the old Waiting Room restored to original Southern style. The museum was also relocated to the gasworks building, where a new and enlarged display made use of the additional space available.

Work was about to start on one of the more important aspects of the four-wheel train project. Push-pull set 484, used mainly on the Ventnor West branch was still extant; the brake/control body No.4112 was at Havenstreet, but its trailer No.6369 was without its running gear at Newtown. Consequently, No.4112 was placed on a temporary underframe in February and made ready for restoration. Work commenced in August when IWR No.46 entered traffic. August also saw the new station at Wootton passed for use by the Railway Inspectorate and the first official train was the 2pm from Havenstreet on the 7th.

Top Left: *After serving the community of Freshwater as a bus shelter for many years, the ex-Freshwater, Yarmouth & Newport Railway (FYN) signal box was returned to its original purpose at Wootton.* IWR Collection

Middle Left: *British Railways Class 03 0-6-0DM shunter 03079 is a tight fit on the car deck of MV* St. Helen *bound for Fishbourne on 8th April.* Terry Hastings

Bottom Left: *Here, 4112 is lifted from its home at Gurnard to start a new life on the rails at Havenstreet.* C. P. Whiting

Below: *A selection of tickets printed in house at Havenstreet.*

Inset: *Dennis Harrison and the late-Phil Lightbown, both retired printers are seen producing a fresh batch of tickets on the company printing press.* Brian Deegan

Of Bricks And Mortarboard

Education has always been a major aspect of the Railway's remit, and Alan Doe and Chris Tagart laboured long in this direction. In association with the local Teacher Centre, they produced an excellent station trail and schools' data pack expressly intended as major teaching aids to visiting groups. These publications were to be the backbone of the educational facility for many years and later coupled with workshop visits provided an excellent product. Educational visits were perhaps not best personified by the BBC TV's *Grange Hill* team, who filmed on 13th September; however the railway looked great on film and the Island as a holiday destination no doubt benefited.

Another part of the commitment was to promote opportunities for educating young and unemployed people with work skills and as such various Manpower Services Commission schemes were started. These groups undertook the rebuilding of the old gasworks at Havenstreet and the completely new museum/administration building. However, probably partly due to lack of management by the Railway these

Above: *W8 now reverted back to a previous life as FYN No.2, and is seen in that company's striking two-tone green livery.* IWR Collection

projects were to become quite costly. The front and back walls of the shop had to be re-built by contractors and considerable defects were found in the workmanship of the new museum. Work came to a standstill at the start of 1987, and after a lengthy period, the local building inspectors recommended that the structure be demolished because the amount of remedial work needed far outweighed that so far completed; all of which proved that there is no such thing as a free lunch!

Things were not particularly happy in Toyland, but a couple of fillips were in train. The Association of Railway Preservation Societies awarded Havenstreet the Premier Award for Best Restored Station in 1987. Station Inspector Chris Tagart went on to praise "our paint supplier who mixes up small quantities of paint to specifications to ensure we have the right shade of green"; now how many times have we heard that in preservation?

Top Left: *The Educational Datapack developed for the 'school party business', which provided teachers with an excellent aid to make the most of a visit to the railway.* Simon Futcher

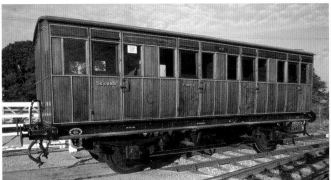

Middle Left: *IWR No.46 in original teak finish in traffic after winning the ARPS award for best restored carriage.* Fincom Holdings/IWR Collection

Bottom Left: *Soon after its arrival D2059 is pressed into service with a demonstration goods train at Smallbrook Junction. The third vehicle in the train is ex-LBSCR cattle van No. 53374, owned by the NRM and placed on loan to us. This wagon was used latterly on the Island for the conveyance of passenger luggage in advance.* IWR Collection

Wootton station also went on to receive a Special Commendation in the 1987 Best Restored Station Competition. Not to be outdone, the four-wheel section of the Carriage & Wagon Department, under the leadership of Pete Jardine, took the ARPS Best Restored Carriage Award for IWR No.46. This was certainly well deserved, as it was, showing the way to numerous other lines in the 'how to do it' stakes.

On 4th August, a Railway team went to Waterloo Station with the English Tourist Board to discuss with British Rail a feasibility study to extend the line to Smallbrook. This was largely as a result of previous discussions between Chris Green, Director Network SouthEast, our Chairman Stuart Page and Marketing Director Jim Loe, where it was suggested that such a scheme could only be seen as beneficial to both railways. The ETB draft feasibility report was received in the Spring of 1988 and an Extension Working Group set up to consider its recommendations. Meanwhile major track renewals were taking place between Havenstreet and Wootton to bring the line up to a higher standard and hopefully reduce maintenance; this would be particularly important if a further **three-and-a-half mile**s was going to come on stream.

A further Class 03 diesel shunter arrived for Network SouthEast on 30th June and the same transporter was used the following day to take W8 Freshwater to a special gala day at Portsmouth & Southsea station to celebrate the re-opening of the re-built high-level platform. Following the singling of the Brading - Sandown section, British Rail agreed to dispose of one and a half miles of track to the Steam Railway and with this, it was full steam ahead for the extension to Smallbrook.

On the Carriage & Wagon front, the LBSCR Brake Third (No.4168) was withdrawn from traffic and there was a certain irony in the words of C&W's Kim Chalkley, when he wrote: "Members need not fear that this vehicle will be forgotten," however, today, 18-years on, it is still out of traffic! To mark the Centenary of the Freshwater, Yarmouth & Newport Railway on 23rd July, W8 was repainted in that railway's bright green livery and re-numbered No.2. Also in the works was a BR Class 03, (D2059), which had arrived on 4th November, after being purchased as a 'Thunderbird' locomotive in event of steam failure on the soon-to-be-extended line.

In January, gangs made their way to Brading to recover the track and some signalling equipment from the singled section on the BR line. Further loads were to come in March from Sandown. These recovered materials were delivered direct to the site on the extension to prevent double handling.

On 13th August 1989, W11 finally returned to traffic after 14-years on the Island, its place was promptly taken by *Ajax* (16-years waiting), which was 'shopped' following asbestos removal at Wootton in May. Ryde Pier Tramcar No.2, or what remained of it, was moved from long-term storage on the Ashey siding (mainline east of Havenstreet), to even longer-term storage in a secure area at the rear of workshops joining other vehicles also awaiting their fate.

For some years the IW Steam Railway had purchased Edmondson card ticket stock from BR at Crewe and tickets were based on traditional mainline railway design. With the imminent closure of the BR printing works, the opportunity was taken to acquire two ticket printing machines and a vast quantity of blank ticket stock, all of which was moved to Havenstreet. Subsequently tickets have been designed and printed in-house, although some stock was bought in during 1991 when large quantities were required urgently for the opening of the Smallbrook extension, when the opportunity was taken to introduce a new style of ticket. Returns were based on the later upright Southern Railway design, whilst singles went back to the original Isle of Wight Railway pattern. On-train issues were designed around the 'Rail Motor Car' type, but machine tickets subsequently replaced these. All that aside, one can certainly commend the IW Steam Railway as continuing the best traditions of the old card ticket devised so long ago on the Newcastle & Carlisle Railway; proving, if we need to, that not all railway preservation is about locomotives, carriages and wagons!

On Island Line the first of the 1938 replacement ex-LT cars arrived on 5th July 1989 and unit 001 was used in a publicity jamboree on the 13th July introducing the 'new' stock. It made a special call at Smallbrook to unveil a banner identifying the site of a new station, 'Due to Open in 1991'. Dare I report that some of us heard the scoffs and sniggers from the 'professional' railwaymen at this display, but then again we had also heard the same thing in 1965, and 1971. Perhaps these same people may not have been so vociferous if they knew of the Isle of Wight Steam Railways ambitions with respect to the Island Line franchise.

Top Right: Newport *returns to its former glory as IWCR No.11.* IWR Collection

Middle Right: *New stock for Island Line was introduced by a banner-breaking exercise at Ryde Pier Head with amongst others, the Network SouthEast Director Chris Green (right), holding the pieces.* Roger Silsbury

Bottom Right: *BR Island Manager, John Winkles and then IW Railway Chairman, Stuart Page, unveil a sign at Smallbrook proclaiming our aims.* Roger Silsbury

SMALLBROOK OR BUST

After years of dreaming, hoping, praying and planning, work on the extension was formally started on 25th August 1989 when our friendly Network SouthEast Director, Chris Green, ceremoniously drove in a key or two on the first length of track heading towards Smallbrook Junction. Meetings with many local and national businesses around this time were very beneficial financially, with many promises turning into tangible forms of support. The timing of the building of the Smallbrook extension was very fortunate, knowing what we know now about the recent history of the railway industry. We had in Chris Green a very great ally, who kindly used influence and pulled strings that frankly we could only have dreamt of before his involvement. He promised that BR would undertake to build an interchange station at Smallbrook Junction and true to his word they did!

The recovered track materials from Sandown were to come in very handy; the extension was progressing very well and by November the first major goal was reached, the overbridge at Rowlands lane. Situated over half a mile from Havenstreet, Rowlands Bridge was the first major structure to be reached by the re-laying gang and a real sense of pride was felt by all involved. Indeed, it was very special to look over the parapet wall and see railway lines instead of vegetation.

Above: *With track again under Rowlands Lane bridge after an absence of 20-years W24* Calbourne *was used to make sure gauging was correct and as its chimney is still intact, it must have been right! Incidentally a lot of structures on the Island system were built to very tight loading gauge and this is why standard size vehicles were never seriously considered when replacing stock in 1966.* Terry Hastings

Whilst the expanding of the railway was very desirable, it led to more demands on all departments! For instance the mechanical engineers would need more engines, and in turn this meant more servicing and additional storage space. With that in mind a reorganisation of the locomotive yard and the construction of a second inspection pit was undertaken in March 1990. Another milestone in carriage preservation was achieved in April 1990 when LCDR composite No.6369 arrived at the railway from Newtown. This body was the missing half of push pull set No.484 and was in exceptional condition considering that it was used as a summerhouse for 52 years. Incredibly, the majority of its seating was still in place, along with all the advertisements and mirrors. The first class compartment also had luggage racks, striking plates, ashtrays and window blinds in place. No structural alterations had been made nor interior painting done to any part of the coach, which was truly astonishing given the vehicle's age.

Other acquisitions were the missing part of LCDR Bogie Third No.2418 (the railway had already acquired the other part), and a Southern Railway bogie scenery van No.TDB 975967 (S4605S). This was ostensibly obtained for the underframe, but it was initially used on extension works trains and latterly as a wood store. Talking of the extension, April 1990 saw the first steam locomotive back at Ashey when Terrier W11 worked a ballast train from Rowlands Lane. A big push in March/April saw 1,200-tons of bottom ballast laid, whilst track materials were assembled from storage along the formation, allowing Ashey to be reached on Sunday 14th April. This was as far as the ex-Sandown track materials stretched, the remainder of the extension would be constructed with redundant materials from Farnham tip, after the singling of the Alton-Farnham line.

In all, 132 60' track panels were purchased from British Rail, and these were stacked up to 20 in a pile (over 20' high), so this was not a walk in the park by any means! A preliminary trip by a gang, complete with 50-ton crane, enabled the stacks to be reduced to manageable heaps of five or six panels. The main onslaught commenced in late June, all the panels were dismantled and the component parts transported to the Island, being laid along the trackbed approximately where they would be required. All this work was done in only eight days, by using an average team of six volunteers per day. The transport of this material was arranged by John and Dave Antell, long-term supporters of the railway and preserved railway haulage specialists, who proved they could move anything from bullhead rail to Bulleid locomotives, plus everything in between.

The Railway was celebrating again in March 1990, when it won the prestigious 'Ian Allan Independent Railway of the Year Award' for 1989. Our Chairman, John Suggett and long-term member Kim Chalkley accepted the award at a presentation ceremony from Ian Allan and the then chairman of British Rail, Sir Robert Reid. More filming took place at Havenstreet and along the line towards Wootton in the Spring of 1990 when sequences for the *Last Train Home* were captured for posterity. Yet another vehicle arrived in March 1990 when ex-LSWR 'Ironclad' 752 (latterly ADS70014) was acquired mainly for its underframe. It was used as a Mechanical Engineers store/workshop during its last years for BR, and as such the body was thought ideal for conversion into a new PW headquarters, but more of this later.

EXTENSIONS & EXITS

The early 1990s were a time of sad goodbyes and cheery celebrations on the Isle of Wight Railway. Firstly there was the sad news of the death of A. B. MacLeod, on 3rd August 1990 at the age of 90. As described earlier, Mr MacLeod was appointed Assistant for the Isle of Wight in charge of locomotives, carriages and wagons in 1928; he later took over the traffic and commercial departments as well, and was instrumental in trying to preserve Beyer Peacock W13. His time on the Island saw many notable achievements including the enlargement of the 02 coal bunkers, improvements to coaching stock and the implementation of a famous East - West through service called 'The Tourist', between Shanklin and Freshwater in 1932. In 1934 this highly popular summer service was extended to start at Ventnor still continuing to Freshwater via Sandown and Newport. His railway career had commenced in 1919 at the Brighton Works under L. B. Billinton and after his stint on the Island he held various positions with the Southern Railway and later British Railways. He finished his career with BR as a Supplies & Contracts Manager in 1964.

His interest for the IW Steam Railway brought him to the Island on many different occasions, but in later years he found the trip from his home in Wimbledon too difficult. Yet, even though he could no longer visit, he still willingly gave advice on liveries and details, which ensured our accuracy in the preservation attempts. His enthusiasm, advice and assistance was invaluable to the Railway especially in the early years and this distinguished railwayman (probably the most significant figure in the history of the Island's railway) would be sadly missed. It was particularly sad that he did not live long enough to see the extension open and a steam train standing at Smallbrook once again. His generosity continued after his passing, as many articles were bequeathed to the railway in his will and these are now included in the collection of railway artefacts at the museum.

Ashey station was the focus of attention during late-1990 and early-1991, as many years of neglect (especially of the drainage system) had to be corrected. The area around Ashey is mainly clay soil and the last years of British Railways ownership saw problems of earth movement and bad drainage lead to the closure of the original station platform due to subsidence. A new short platform and shelter were built on the south (down) side of the formation in 1961 to serve the sparse community until closure in 1966. After becoming derelict, maintenance of the drainage ceased and within a few years flooding of the formation became the norm.

Top Left: *Alastair MacLeod at Havenstreet in August 1975.* John Goss

Bottom Left: *Track laying on the extension is seen here progressing well towards Ashey.* IWR Collection

Top Right: *Easter Monday 1991 when W11 reached Smallbrook with the first steam hauled train for 25-years.* D. Walker

Our engineers had to clear the old formation of vegetation, remove a large amount of sodden clay, re-build drains and replace the trackbed with tons of chalk in preparation for track laying to begin in earnest on the final section between Smallbrook and Ashey.

Birthday Celebrations came thick and fast in 1991, with no fewer than six landmark events nominated for appropriate bun fights! These included the facts that: our flagship locomotive W24 *Calbourne* was to be 100-years old in December; the Wight Locomotive Society, the forerunner of the present company had been formed 25-years before on the 28th April; the last BR steam-hauled passenger train ran 25-years ago on the 31st December; our Hawthorn Leslie 0-4-0ST *Invincible* had arrived 20-years previously on the 3rd June; and finally (and probably most important of all) we would see the scheduled opening of the extension between Havenstreet and Smallbrook in July.

With so many celebrations coming up it would prove to be a very busy year for the staff and volunteers, not only would much sweat and toil be needed on extension works but important changes were required on the signalling systems at Havenstreet as well.

Operating requirements for the new longer railway would mean a lot of training and familiarisation before July, but firstly the infrastructure had to be changed, inspected and hopefully passed fit by the Railway Inspectorate before it could be brought into use. All this to be done and we still had a railway to run to Wootton; it was a tall order for everyone. Could we achieve it? Of course we could!

The final push on the extension came over the Easter weekend 1991, when up to 57 volunteers (all Heinz varieties included) worked to lay the final section from near Smallbrook to Ashey. This amazing weekend was a joy to behold, the enthusiasm was fantastic and track-laying was completed at a phenomenal rate. The final rails were dropped into place on the Easter Monday finally linking up the whole three-and-a-half miles; only the station area at Smallbrook remained to be done. A works train had followed progress during the weekend, moving materials and checking clearances as it went. On the Monday, after working all day it returned to Havenstreet where the diesel locomotive was replaced by steam and amid much celebration, waving and cheering from people along the lineside!

Top Left: *The gang at the boundary fence with Island Line, as a train passes.* Simon Futcher

Middle Left: *Contractors Dyer & Butler completed the two Smallbrook platforms in 11 weeks. Here a team are well on with the decking stage on the Steam Railway platform.* Ray Maxfield

Bottom Left: *Here the Island Line platform nears completion, but this picture is taken from a photographic angle not to be recommended to anyone else!* Ray Maxfield

Thus W11 *Newport* pulled the very first steam train from Havenstreet to Smallbrook for 25-years. and on arriving there (very close to the present station), it was greeted by Island Manager, John Winkles. Whistles were exchanged between W11 and the passing electric trains, entertaining the amazed passengers on their way to Ryde or Shanklin. So attention turned to Smallbrook, where the station site needed to be levelled and a minimum of six inches of chalk spread over the whole formation followed by another six inches of bottom ballast. The actual station construction was started in May by contractors Dyer & Butler of Southampton. They completed the BR side first, before starting on our side, but the whole station was completed in 11 weeks. Meanwhile suitable turnouts were identified at BR's Eastleigh depot and they eventually arrived at the railway in June, after which the final parts of the track jigsaw fell into place. Much hard work and burning of the midnight oil ensued over the next few weeks. The 13-14th July saw the last pieces of pointwork being fitted along with the engine release spur and associated S&T requirements. Work finally finished at 9.30pm on the 14th, with everyone totally exhausted but happy.

The very next day Major Olver of Her Majesty's Railway Inspectorate arrived and travelled up to Smallbrook to inspect the new station, the BR side platform was satisfactory but our side was found to be a little wide to gauge, (sadly it was something we had challenged with BR's engineers from the outset but were overruled). However, this was a distinct disappointment but it was solved later by slewing the track and did not affect the opening. After leaving Smallbrook, Major Olver inspected various areas on the extension finishing with the new signalling arrangements at Havenstreet. Much to our relief he was satisfied with our efforts and gave the go-ahead for passenger services to commence at a line speed of 25mph.

Whilst all this excitement was going on to the east, another four-wheel coach restoration was completed at Havenstreet. As a consequence, LCDR Driving Saloon Brake Third No 4112, the first part of the push-pull set 484, entered traffic on 7th July 1991 just a few days before the extension opened; how was that for timing?

A fond farewell was given to Tiger our 0-4-0 diesel hydraulic locomotive (ex-Esso shunter from Fawley) in June 1991. After working a final works train to Smallbrook and back it was loaded onto John Antell's low-loader and left the Island for a new life at Bo'ness in Scotland. Another bogie coach body, an LBSCR eight-compartment Third (reputed to be SR 2065 of 1903) was acquired.

This coach body had come from Runcton near Chichester in July 1991, and had previously been offered to the Bluebell Railway but they were unable to take it, so after a site visit to assess it's suitability we agreed to bring it to the Island. Even though it never ran on the Island, two identical coaches were employed between 1936 and 1956/59, these being SR No.2410 and No.2411.

Saturday 20th July 1991 was to most people just another day, but to the volunteers, staff and guests of the Isle of Wight Railway Company, it was a very special day indeed; and one that we had been waiting for since way back in our early preservation days. To have a decent length of running line at last, which gave us an interchange station so passengers could access the railway much easier. Furthermore, it would bring another three miles 40 chains of original railway back to doing the job it was designed for and not left idle, unwanted and overgrown, was a dream come true. This was what most people involved in Island railway preservation had signed-up for, to save a part of our railway heritage for posterity and provide enjoyment and education of our visitors. Not only that, but to give them and future generations, a feel of what Island railways had been like before the age of mass motor car ownership had destroyed the need for most rail routes on the Island.

The official Smallbrook Extension opening day arrived, and it was a day full of celebrations. Rightly so, for our project engineering team led by Ian Wightmore and Graham Deegan had built an extension to be proud of. It was amazing how everything had worked out to perfection, cash-flow was masterminded by Nick Boycott, the money had been found without need for massive borrowing, and no financial millstone had been put round the company's neck.

The materials required had been made available at very fair prices, and the expertise and enthusiasm of our volunteers was second to none. As stated earlier, promises from various quarters had been turned into tangible help in many different forms, including the hand-over of the track bed freehold by the IW Council. We had been lucky in our timing, but my word did our volunteers make the most of it and they had every right to feel mightily pleased with themselves. For those readers with a number-crunching bent, the vital statistics that made up our extension story will show that we constructed this line with approximately 30,000 man-hours over a 23-month period. In round terms 800 rails were laid on 7,000 sleepers using 78,000 fastenings, all on around 12,000 tons of ballast. We used Tarmac-laying machines to lay the bottom ballast, a very innovative and un-tested idea by our project leaders, but in practice it worked a dream. The ravages of 25-years dereliction were not ignored, but with an eye to the future all the major engineering hurdles were sorted out properly leaving us with a fairly low-maintenance railway for years to come.

Top Right: *The very first trains to cross at Havenstreet for 25 years. on 21st July 1991.* Iain Whitlam

Bottom Right: *Island Line unit 483 003 and IW Steam Railway W24 Calbourne* break the banner simultaneously to officially open the *Smallbrook extension.* Ray Maxfield

Above: *W8* Freshwater *near Long Arch bridge on the extension to Smallbrook. Shortly after return to traffic with a new boiler in August 1998.* IWR Collection

The day of the extension's opening dawned sunny and warm, a good start for the guests who arrived in plenty of time from such auspicious organisations as the English Tourist Board, Network SouthEast, Wightlink, Local Councils and the Rural Development Commission.

The official opening ceremony was carried out by Mr David Benson, Director of Wightlink. Afterwards the inaugural train left Havenstreet at 11.25am, arriving at Smallbrook at 11.38am, hauled by our flagship and resplendent W24 *Calbourne*. The 11.32am Island Line train from Shanklin, was driven by Ken West (whose regular locomotive in steam days had been W24) and arrived at Smallbrook at 11.48am. The passengers on this service were invited to witness the opening ceremony, on the promise they would not miss their ferry at the Pier Head! After Chris Green, Managing Director of Network SouthEast had officially opened the station, *Calbourne* and the BR train moved forward simultaneously to break banners across both tracks, amid lots of whistling and hooting.

Our train then proceeded at 12.15pm to run non-stop to Wootton and thence back to Havenstreet where our guests, volunteers and staff enjoyed a buffet lunch. The remainder of the day was taken up with regular trips to Smallbrook so that everyone could enjoy the new and exciting ride to our new eastern terminus.

So began a new chapter in the history of the Isle of Wight Railway Company, a seed of a dream that just a small number of enthusiasts had in the 1960s, had finally blossomed into a beautiful and carefully nurtured flower in the 1990s; a heritage railway that had been true to its ideals and really did do what it said on the posters! God bless the few, for without their vision, commitment and enthusiasm then, we wouldn't be writing this now. Over the next few days, as the dust settled, we got used to running our new railway. Everything worked very well, with the staff very quickly coming to terms with the new requirements and coping admirably with the huge upsurge in visitor numbers. As expected, with the headline news of the extension making such illustrious newspapers as the *Daily Telegraph* and the *Daily Mail*, whilst the railway press gave us superb coverage. The subsequent interest from public and enthusiasts alike was both phenomenal and very gratifying, especially after so much hard work achieving our goal.

A well-deserved award was received in early 1992 when the Association of Railway Preservation Societies 'Annual Award' was given in recognition of the most outstanding contribution to railway preservation by an ARPS member organisation during the year. The citation read: 'The 1991 Award is made to the Isle of Wight Railway for re-opening the line from Havenstreet to a new interchange with British Rail at Smallbrook Junction.'

It went on to note the efforts of the volunteers in building the extension and the willing support of BR's Network SouthEast, the English Tourist Board, Wightlink Ferries, the Rural Development Commission and the Island's three local authorities. The news was officially announced at the ARPS Annual General Meeting at Gateshead on Saturday 25th January 1992, and our Chairman, John Suggett received the award on behalf of the Railway along with project engineers Ian Wightmore, Graham Deegan and Neil Rees. The Railway realised even before the extension was completed that it was not only facing a motive power shortage, but also needed larger engines to cope with the heavier trains and the longer distances they ran between servicing stops. Our 02 Class *Calbourne* was the only large engine on our books, and this was proving to be unreliable. Recurring problems with its boiler and firebox meant that we were living on borrowed time and that major work would be needed sooner rather than later. We had embarked on a course of restoration on *Ajax* to respond to this fact, but this was proving to be very problematic. The task was far greater than was first thought and although progress was being made, it was clearly not as quick as required to fill the gap that was opening very fast. It was therefore very fortuitous that a Hunslet 0-6-0ST Austerity type was found to be available for a long-term loan from the Royal Corps of Transport Museum Trust. After negotiations with the Trust, an agreement was reached which allowed us to use the engine for a period of five-years and this also included a loan of a Barclay diesel mechanical 0-4-0 shunter No.253 for a similar period.

The Austerity, *Royal Engineer* was built in 1953 and saw service with the army at Steventon (Berkshire) and Bicester before moving to Long Marston in Warwickshire. Restored in 1970/1. It was overhauled again in 1987/8 and stored by the Royal Corps of Transport Museum Trust awaiting permanent display facilities. It was finally moved to the Island from Long Marston by Haulier John Antell on the 11-12th February, the ferry crossing being sponsored by Wightlink. The diesel shunter No.253 built in 1945 followed closely, arriving on the Island on 14th February.

Top Right: *Army 198* Royal Engineer *touches down at Havenstreet on 12th February 1992.* Terry Hastings

Middle Right: *Buy one – get one free; a Valentine's Day surprise as Army 253 arrives on the 14th February.* Terry Hastings

Bottom Right: *The travelling sales stand is pitched up at the Great Dorset Steam Fayre in August 1991 selling long lost railway titles to the unsuspecting public. It is manned on this occasion by Steve and Yvonne Castle.* Derck Bishop

One of the often-neglected parts of railway preservation is the commitment of some members to create publicity and make money for the cause. In the early days of our society a travelling sales stand was started by selling relics from a table at Clapham Transport Museum. Iain Whitlam (and almost anyone else who was available at the time) manned this, but gradually a more organised sales stand developed under the careful stewardship of Derek Bishop. A large trailer was procured for this purpose and it proceeded to travel far and wide to events all over the country.

Derek continued to bang the drum for the railway for over 20-years showing a commitment of extraordinary tenacity. Derek closed the shutters for the last time in 1991. He had seen off all the other railway societies in the south long before, only the Talyllyn society was still to be seen 'on the road' going to rallies. Being frugal we don't waste anything so the trailer came to Havenstreet and was transformed into Rally Control for our annual Steam Extravaganza event and still continues to be used for this purpose to date. Derek remains committed to supporting the railway and after taking early retirement from his nine-to-five job for a leading bank, he now finds even more diverse ways of helping the railway, from organising a real ale bar to decorating the Christmas grotto.

During the 1990s, the Railway won the ARPS award for the best railway information leaflet twice in succession. Competition was stiff, with all the long-established and wealthier lines taking part. Much of the concept work was 'in-house' and member Brian Masterton actually did all the artwork and production of the second award winning entry. Although *Royal Engineer* had been in use for a while, a ceremony was held on 12th June 1992 when Brigadier David Kinnear officially 'handed over' the locomotive to the Railway on a five-year lease. Members of Alistair MacLeod's family were entertained at the Railway in June, having a trip in the restored four-wheeler 4112 and a conducted tour of the facilities at Havenstreet. Mr MacLeod's son Ewan and his daughter Alison also unveiled a relief map of the Isle of Wight in the Waiting Room, which had been restored with part of the bequest that 'Mac' had left the Railway in his will. This map is still displayed in the Waiting Room at Havenstreet and continues to look splendid.

Calbourne had been stopped with axlebox problems since February but took to the rails again in early June 1992, but sadly after only 16-days in traffic, serious cracks were found in the copper firebox. A decision was made to stop the locomotive for its ten-year overhaul early thus putting the onus of all heavy peak service trains onto *Royal Engineer*, which happily was performing very well. Another filming session came to the Railway on 25th July when some scenes for Ken Russell's adaptation of *Lady Chatterley* were captured at Havenstreet. A number of staff were called upon to become extras but none had more steamier parts than W8 *Freshwater*! The last of the 'new' 1938 tube stock arrived on the Island in the shape of unit 009 entering service on 15th June. This led to the withdrawal of the final three cars of 'Standard' stock, thus another part of Island railway history came to an end.

Above: Freshwater *was a late replacement for the failed* Calbourne *and found fame in Ken Russell's film adaptation of the novel* Lady Chatterley. IWR Collection

As 1991 closed, a tally of the passenger journeys made during the year taken from the guard's journals showed a figure of 100,016. This was the first time a figure of over 100,000 journeys had been recorded on the railway, and it proved what a worthwhile project the extension had been for both the good of the railway and its future financial security. Our new locomotive *Royal Engineer* was fitted out with Westinghouse air brake equipment shortly after its arrival and was pressed into use appropriately for the May visit of Major Olver from the Railway Inspectorate. This visit was to look at the outstanding items left over from his original inspection; including the gauging of the platform at Smallbrook after slewing of the track to correct the earlier problems.

Above: *Ashey Halt transformed for filming the BBC's* Return of the Psammead. Terry Hastings

THE OLD ORDER CHANGETH

As 1993 dawned, the prospect of BR Privatisation was causing the Railway concern, so Jim Loe, our Commercial Director was asked to co-ordinate the Railway's part in future developments. All the talks at this time were treated as confidential, so very little information was passed to the membership. However, the Railway was keenly aware that a lot of traffic was now being generated from the new Smallbrook station, so a say in what happened to the BR Island line was certainly seen as a responsible stance to take. What we should do about the Island Line franchise was up to the Board of Directors, but the feeling was that we should not be frightened to go for it and talk was all about how we should do it rather than if we should. As is often said, watch this space….

Meanwhile, on 24th January 1993 came a very sad occasion with the death of Sir Peter Allen, Patron of the Isle of Wight Railway and a Vice-President of the erstwhile Wight Locomotive Society. He had been born at Ashtead, Surrey on 8th September 1905 and after graduating from college in 1928 joined Brunner Mond, one of the firms that merged to form Imperial Chemical Industries.

Sir Peter remained with ICI throughout his career, and was appointed a Director in 1951. He rose to become Chairman in 1968, a post he held until retirement in 1971; he was then knighted in 1967 for services to his industry. He became familiar with the Island before World War I, when family holidays were taken here and his fascination for the unique railway system stayed with him throughout his life.

As mentioned earlier Sir Peter was instrumental in both the A1X 'Terrier' locomotives returning to the Island, having successfully negotiated deals with both Butlin's and Whitbread on behalf of the Railway. He also very generously paid for the transport costs of returning W11 *Newport* from North Wales and for the repainting costs to Isle of Wight Central livery. Sadly, by the time W11 returned to traffic, he was unable to make the journey to the Island from his home in Battle but a special telephone link enabled him to participate in the ceremony. The Railway was always 'his favourite railway' and he was ever generous in support, using his influence and contributing financially on many occasions. His presence would be sadly missed!

Top Left: *Neil Rees is seen in this picture, whilst fitting new bed-plates for the bunker and cab area on W24* Calbourne *on 19th January 1993.* Brian Deegan

Bottom Left: *At Smallbrook a ground-frame box was erected using parts from Whitwell signal box, the sign above the door is a replica based upon the one on the original box.* IWR Collection

The recession of the early 1990s was beginning to bite and although our trading was seen as quite good, compared to some Island tourist attractions, it was clear that tough times were ahead. Overhaul work on *Calbourne* was progressing well with the boiler out and frames laid bare. This gave us the opportunity to replace the 'MacLeod' larger bunker, as much metal work around the 'back end' had to be renewed due to 'wastage'. The old LSWR design of bunker was to be reinstated with additional coal rails, so that an early version of the Southern livery could be applied when the overhaul was completed. The larger bunker was to be stored and refitted on a future overhaul.

The signalling arrangements at Smallbrook are very basic, but even a simple layout requires the provision of two levers; a lever to move the single line points and another to lock the points in position, known as a Facing Point Lock (FPL). This is provided by a two-lever ground-frame, which is unlocked by the Single Line Tablet released at Havenstreet signal box and then carried on the locomotive. This arrangement is quite normal and the equipment is happy to live outside in the weather without coming to any harm and this it did for a while.

However, it was felt that a little bit of covered accommodation would keep the staff dry whilst running the engine round its train and this would also make the place seem a little more business-like. A suitable building was erected during the early part of 1993, using sections of a waiting room built at Ashey by the BBC for filming *Return of the Psammead*, along with parts of a garden shed that had once been the lower section of Whitwell Signal box. The back wall, one side and the door were all original items from the signalling equipment manufacturers Saxby & Farmer, and the whole lot was assembled by some labour on an employment-training scheme. The new 'box' came into use in April 1993 and continues to provide shelter to pointsmen or train crew whilst they operate the point.

As privatisation plans were being bandied around on BR's Island line, we learned that a shadow franchise would soon start, as this would be one of the first sections to be privatised. A special case of vertical integration was also talked about for the Ryde-Shanklin line, this meaning that instead of Railtrack owning and running the infrastructure, the operating company would look after the whole lot, trains, track and signalling. What a good idea! Whilst all this hot air was circulating around the meetings tables, Ryde Works were busy repainting all the new Class 483 ex-LT stock into the new corporate Network SouthEast colours, but was this an ominous sign? There was an old railway tradition, that if the paint pot came out to change a colour scheme, it usually meant it was either shortly going to change again or it was going to be shut down!

Work had been going on steadily, completing the many jobs that had to be finished on the extension to Smallbrook in order to reach the correct standard. The whole line had been laid on good firm ballast but even this settles, so many hours of laborious sleeper packing had to be carried out. Work on drainage, fencing, lineside clearance and level crossing work had not been finished in 1991 and had taken many months to get right. Ashey station was also on the list waiting to be finished and this was done during early 1993. This station was never seen as a priority, for it was as remote then as it was when the railway first opened way back in 1875, but the Railway was committed to see it in use again. The station house had been sold as a private dwelling thus all that remained to re-open was a short platform and a small brick waiting shelter. After many months of waiting, the first passenger train to stop at Ashey Halt since closure in 1966 was the 10am Havenstreet to Smallbrook service on 2nd May 1993; with this, yet another rung on the preservation ladder was reached.

The Island's railway heritage had been slowly disappearing over the years with station sites, trackbed and structures all succumbing to new housing, road improvements or the like. Another part was lost in May 1993 when the last surviving piece of Cowes station was demolished to make way for a new Co-op supermarket. Sadly the Cowes station site was to become totally unrecognisable with all vestiges of railway activity gone for good, following the fate of many of the stations on the Island. On a more positive note the ex-LCDR Composite Saloon No.6369 entered traffic on 18th July 1993. This was the missing part of the push-pull set No.484 and it was tremendously rewarding to see both carriages back together, and looking superb with the gangway in place. The sight of these two restored four-wheelers being pulled by a Terrier locomotive really did bring home the fact that we had revived a bygone era of Island transport.

Set 484 was once in regular use on both the Ventnor West branch and the Bembridge branch and now it would be a regular performer on the Smallbrook to Wootton line. What a fantastic achievement this was to recreate a scene that disappeared from railway history way back in the mists of time when bogie coaches replaced the four-wheeler. Although these new bogie carriages brought with them more space, better riding at speed, and quiet comfort for the passenger; in a few locations (including the Island) the four-wheeler had enjoyed an extension to their working lives. Not only did our four-wheel coaches portray what a Victorian railway looked like, but they also give our passengers the feel of how rough the ride would have been for the early travellers, especially on a long journey. They had none of the luxuries of suspension, nor even soft springs or toilets, and you couldn't even stroll up to the buffet for a bite to eat or a cuppa; it was basic cross your legs, grit your teeth and sit tight till you arrived at your destination. At least our journey is short and the passengers can still enjoy the four-wheel experience without the discomforts of the past.

Right: *The basic station facilities were brought back into use at Ashey in May 1993, here W24* Calbourne *with a train of four-wheel coaches calls at the halt.* IWR Collection

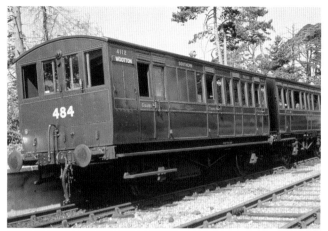

Top Left: *Pictured here at Wootton in August 1993, we find push-pull set No.484 once again graces the rails of the Island after the superb restoration of four-wheelers 4112 and 6369.* Terry Hastings

Middle Left: *Here we have an interior view showing passenger accommodation in set No.484.* IWR Collection

Bottom Left: *Next we have a further view of set No.484, this time one showing the interior of the driving compartment.* D Walker

As the years rolled by, more and more of the old Island railwaymen were passing away, many of whom had given the fledgling Society a great deal of help in the early days. One such stalwart was Syd Newbery, who passed away on 19th June 1993 aged 83. Syd worked on the Island railways for 50-years and was latterly the Permanent Way Supervisor at Ryde, retiring in 1975. When the Society was feeling its way in the early days, Syd was happy to give help unstintingly on all aspects of permanent way work. He regularly gave his time and came to walk the line with Jim Loe (then our PW ganger) pointing out faults and how to rectify them, and always entertaining with tales of happier times on the Island system. I was also to meet Syd on many occasions when I was latterly in charge of PW matters, and although not a well man he still freely passed on his wisdom and knowledge, and still had a good few tales to tell to boot.

Another with 49-years of service behind him, driver Ken West retired on 15th September 1993, when he drove his last electric train for BR. Ken had started as a cleaner at Newport shed on 23rd July 1944, progressing via a fireman to become the regular driver of 02 Class W24 *Calbourne* in the 1960s. Ken had a remarkable career, working on the last Terriers based at Newport, driving the last train out of Cowes and the first electric train in 1967. He also drove *Calbourne* on the last day of steam on a Locomotive Club of Great Britain special. After retiring, Ken started driving for the Steam Railway, and over the years he passed on his skill and expertise to many of our younger drivers. Ken was driving the first train to stop at the newly opened Ashey station and how appropriate it was considering that he was the driver of the last BR train to make a scheduled stop there in 1966.

Not only was Ken kind enough to volunteer to do driving turns for us, but over the years it became a bit of a family affair. Margaret, Ken's wife, ran the Refreshment Room for many years until retirement, whilst his daughter Liz joined the Railway as a young volunteer and still works regularly on special events and Guard duties. Liz married Chris Tagart a few years ago, also a long-term volunteer and then a Director, so his duties as fireman gave the opportunity for a total train crew of family members! Even the couple's young daughters are growing up as helpers on the Railway and will hopefully carry on the tradition for a few years to come. Sadly the end of the 2004 season saw Ken hang up his grease-top cap for the last time, although still very fit and active, he thought the time had come to leave engine-driving to the younger chaps. The banter and stories from the enginemen's mess would never be the same without Ken, his cheerfulness and singing as he oiled round in the mornings was a joy to behold. But all good things must come to an end and we thank Ken for his help over the years.

As 1994 arrived we outshopped one of the drop-side wagons, No.483700, fully refurbished as Hocknulls Coal & Coke No.1. Although this was not a firm that had private owner wagons back in the good old days on the Island, we had developed a good partnership with Hocknulls as they supplied our locomotive coal. They also sponsored the re-building and re-painting of the wagon in return for the advertising opportunity the wagon sides afford when on show in the public areas.

The Railway got the cheque book out again for another purchase of rolling stock in 1994. We bought four pipe wagon underframes from the Royal Navy Armaments Depot at Bedenham, Gosport for future use with Oldbury four-wheel coach bodies. These were Nos. B740232, B741157, B741382 and B741934, which are still in store awaiting restoration.

The start of the 1994 season saw a once regular Island event, Ashey Races, restored to the calendar. At one time these were a huge attraction, with the pony racing bringing crowds of people from all over the Island. Many travelled by special trains and were treated to a grandstand view from the carriages as they were shunted round the chalk pit siding, as this offered a great view of the racecourse. Sadly over the years the races fell out of favour and the crowds dwindled, the chalk pit siding was removed and the fields returned to agricultural use.

Early in the 1990s a group of local farmers and interested parties resurrected the 'scurry' as modern day parlance describes it. It attracted so much public interest that the organisers asked if the Railway could get involved. Ashey Station having been re-opened could be used to get some members of the public to the racing and this was agreed for 1994. The 'scurry' was held on Sunday March 20th and a surprisingly large amount of race-goers used the train to travel to Ashey making it well worthwhile running the trains. Since then it has proved to be an annual event and the Railway has provided the public with an alternative to having to drive their cars down very bumpy tracks and park in muddy fields; the Railway even has its own race, with the IW Railway Cup going to the winner!

On 1st April 1994 (some may say a most appropriate date) Network SouthEast ceased to exist, as the splitting up of the country's rail network began, with shadow franchises taking control of various business sectors, as laid down in the Railway Act 1993. Island Line was to be offered as a 'stand alone' franchise and as such a shadow franchise management team was put in place under the control of a Director, Dominic Booth. Once again the Island railway was unique, as the signalmen would work for Island Line unlike all other signalmen in the country who now worked for Railtrack. Although initially Island Line was planned to be one of the first franchises to be let, it was eventually deferred and not even included in the second round of sell-offs.

Top Right: *Ken West, one of the real stalwarts of the Isle of Wight Steam Railway is seen here on W24* Calbourne, *his regular engine from BR days.* Jeff Layfield

Bottom Right: *Newly restored drop-side wagon No.483700 masquerades as Hocknulls No.1 pictured at Wootton. In reality, this is a fictitious livery, but it was done in return for all the support the Cowes-based coal merchants have given the Railway.* IWR Collection

Meanwhile a consortium had been formed between Southern Vectis, Wightlink and Hovertravel, all of whom had a natural interest in operating the line. The Steam Railway was not a member, but nevertheless it was invited to meetings as we had the knowledge of railway matters that the rest were lacking. It was all very interesting, but somehow disconcerting at the same time, and all we could do was continue to watch the drama unfold and prepare our case.

The end of the early electric era happened in April when the final four vehicles of 'Standard' stock were scrapped at Sandown yard. After removal of conductor shoes at Ryde Works, the vehicles were hauled to Sandown by a class 483 unit and berthed in the former Newport line bay. An approved contractor from Wales then had to build a special shed to remove asbestos before the final scrapping took place. The final four cars were Numbers 5, 26, 28 and 31, each pushed in turn into the stripping shed by Island Line diesel shunter 03079, after which the remains were dealt with swiftly in the sidings. All the cars had been scrapped by 25th April. Incidentally car No.26 was actually the first ex-LT vehicle of the 'new' electric fleet to arrive on the Island way back in 1966 and thus one of the last to leave, albeit in bits!

Below: *The railway's A1X Class W11* Newport *had been repainted into lined black livery with the British Railways early crest in April 1994 and numbered 32640. It was given a Fratton shed-plate (70F) and a cast number plate on the smokebox, and very smart it looked too. Also in the paint shop was D2059 (alias* Edward*), whose green BR livery gave way to a nice shiny black one; did we buy too much Dulux for Newport?* IWR Collection

As June 1994 came round, we had a visit from the then Minister of Public Transport, the Right Hon. Roger Freeman MP, who was accompanied by Barry Field the local Member of Parliament, and an entourage of secretarial staff. This meeting was organised by the consortium to discuss the Island Line franchise, and we offered to host it. Much of the talk was around the way the franchise would be let and how Island Line would remain a public transport entity rather than being sold off to the private sector.

Having repainted W11, we had the embarrassing situation of withdrawing it from service after a very short time. Leaking tubes had got progressively worse and after a few spot renewals the repairs were insufficient to rectify the problem. The locomotive would need a complete re-tube and possibly further boiler work. This left only two serviceable steam locomotives to carry on the main bulk of the season's trains and careful planning was needed to make sure services continued uninterrupted' thankfully all went well and the 1994 season carried on with no disruption.

Another of the Oldbury IWR coach bodies (believed to be No.35) was moved about four miles from St. Helens to Havenstreet in September 1994. Although the body had been donated in 1993, no attempt was made to move it until the ground conditions at the site improved. The body was in a very poor condition and as such was seen as a very long-term project. The same camp site was also home to another Oldbury body, a full Third, the only known survivor, but it was unfortunately a total wreck having collapsed some years before. The Railway did manage to salvage a door or two and a complete set of grab rails, hinges and door handles, but the rest was simply burnt.

Matters Maritime

Any readers who had travelled to the Island during steam days and electric days up to the 1980s will no doubt have a mental picture of the passenger ferry crossing from Portsmouth Harbour to Ryde Pier Head. The Denny-built diesel ferries, named *Brading*, *Southsea* and *Shanklin* were held in great affection by almost all their passengers and the staff. The first two *Brading* and *Southsea* had been ordered in SR days to replace two vessels lost during World War II, but due to post-war supply shortages did not arrive until British Railways had taken over. Always known as the 'Denny twins', they were launched on 11th March 1948 in Dumbarton. In a ceremony by Mrs O. V. Bulleid, No.1412 *Brading* followed *Southsea*, No 1411 into the water. *Southsea* had been christened some 30-minutes earlier by the wife of Sir John Elliot, Chief Regional Officer of the Southern Region of BR.

The *Shanklin* was delivered in 1951 and although very similar, it had various alterations to the Sulzer engines, unfortunately these were not as reliable as those in the older boats and made for problems in later operation. The diesels plied the route along with the remaining paddle steamers, but their reliability and capacity (they were licensed for 1,330

Above: *During a refit programme in 1966/67, MV* Shanklin *underwent major surgery on hatches and shell doors, including the addition of a new spar deck. This view taken early in the process was taken in Southampton where our Isle of Wight 'liner' shares the docks with some bigger sisters.* Terry Hastings

passengers) soon meant that several 'paddlers' were withdrawn, the last being PS *Ryde*. This vessel was withdrawn from service in 1969 and sold for further use as a nightclub at Binfield on the River Medina. Sadly the years have not been kind to it, for after being gutted twice by fire, at the time of writing *Ryde* is little more than a rusted hulk, condemned by the local authorities as a dangerous structure; a sad end to a World War II veteran.

The Denny diesel ships had been slightly altered over the years, but essentially they remained the same and millions of holidaymakers and commuters alike loved their comfort and reliability. They ran in almost any weather after radar was fitted, the crossing time always gave good connections either side of the Spithead and provided a lovely half hour of either relaxed comfort below decks or a thoroughly good cobweb-blowing session on the main or upper decks.

I think it is safe to say everyone was sad to see them go following the advent of the 'new' high-speed catamaran service. Many hoped that some if not all of them would find new owners and a new lease of life elsewhere, indeed *Shanklin* did find alternative work. As mentioned earlier this vessel was a little more unreliable than the others and was consequently the first to be laid up in 1980. The Paddle Steamer Preservation Group (owners of the well-known PS *Waverley*) bought it with a view to using her as a cruising vessel. It returned to its birthplace on the Clyde for repairs, after which it was re-named *Prince Ivanhoe* and started work as a cruise ship in the Bristol Channel in the 1981 season. It was to be a short-lived career change as it unfortunately came to grief after running onto an uncharted object near the South Wales coast. The ship was beached off Port Eynon and thankfully there was no direct loss of life, although a member of the Paddle Steamer Society suffered a fatal heart attack during the emergency. After an assessment of the damage, it was found to be so great that the ship was declared a loss!

Brading and *Southsea* continued in service until 1986 when the then owners, Sea Containers, introduced the new Australian-built catamarans. *Brading* was cannibalised for spares and sold for re-use or scrap. Although several attempts to save the ship were started, nothing came of them and after several moves it was towed to Pound's Shipbreaking yard at Tipner in Portsmouth Harbour. Only a matter of yards away from the M275, many people must have seen *Brading* in the final few years gradually losing all dignity as its paint gave way to rust. It was in October of 1994 that it finally met its end; the demise was spectacular for whilst cutting with oxy-acetylene torches, *Brading* caught fire. Controlled burning was allowed by the fire brigade, allowing flames of up to 60' to give the passing motorists a spectacular sight as it turned into a charred hulk. The cutting started once it was found to be safe enough to do so and that was the end of *Brading*; meanwhile *Southsea* had a very long and lingering demise. Kept on by Sealink (Sea Containers) as a spare boat after the new high-speed service began, it did a little cruising work but was eventually retired in 1989. Many attempts to save this boat were made and it was moved from pillar to post, as different schemes came and went, and it spent time at Newhaven, Falmouth, Bristol, Southampton and Portsmouth to name but a few.

Time in storage never does a ship much good and things had got to a pretty bad state, but it still came as something of a surprise to find that it was sold by the owners at very short notice to a Danish Shipbreaking yard. It was towed to Esbjerg arriving in March 2005 for dismantling and so the saga ends. **None of us can experience the joy of gazing down one of the engine room access points, listening to the rhythmic beat of the Sulzer engines, feeling the blasts of hot air rising from below and breathing in that rich aroma of diesel and hot lubrication oils.**

Top Left: *PS* Ryde *attracts scant interest as it goes astern from the south end of Portsmouth Harbour pier in 1968.* Terry Hastings

Bottom Left: *The paddle steamer* Ryde *remained coal-fired until its final day. In later years, in order to bunker the ship a barge was put alongside the sponson and sacks of coal craned on board. Here Fireman Ted Stray is cleaning the fire in one of the stokeholes.* Terry Hastings

MV Southsea *fresh from refit in March 1984 makes a fine sight heading for Ryde.* Terry Hastings

A final ignominy, as the remains of PS Ryde *are seen derelict, and dangerous on 8th September 2004.* Matt Birkin

LEARNING THE FACTS OF LIFE, THE HARD WAY

Above: *Terence Cuneo pictured at Havenstreet during his visit on 6th November.* Brian Deegan

After taking a trip down memory lane with the Island's BR ferries, we must now return to the Railway's story. Before we reached the end of 1994 we had a very unexpected, but highly appreciated visit from Terence Cuneo CVO, OBE, RGI, FGRA on 1st November. This well-known and respected railway artist had been staying in the Edward VII convalescent home at Osborne and as a birthday surprise his daughter Carol had arranged a special 'behind the scenes' visit to the Railway. The Railway then provided another surprise by arranging for him to be guest of honour on Sunday 6th November, when he was given a first class trip by steam accompanied by Director Brian Bell. Although he was then aged 87 he was still tremendously enthusiastic about railways and took a real interest in what we were doing. In return Mr Cuneo gave us a copy of one of his paintings and this now hangs in the company offices. Sadly Terence Cuneo passed away in 1996 but his work lives on and many people will be familiar with his paintings of such diverse subjects as portraits of Royalty, industrial scenes and (of course} railways. His railway pictures, many done on commissions to British Railways showing modernisation subjects; all had the Cuneo trade-mark of a little mouse hidden away in each of the paintings.

The 1994 season was a difficult year with locomotive problems really coming to the fore, nevertheless we had a good trading year bucking the trend of the last couple and producing more passenger journeys than 1993 despite reducing the number of operating days from 143 to 140. The recession had bitten but not too badly and the signs were looking more promising. The on-going saga of Island Line privatisation rumbled on with a statement from the Office of Passenger Rail Franchising that it would be at least 1996, if not 1997 before the Island service would be franchised. The Railway's Board of Directors had by this time been working on proposals and had decided that a bid would be made for running Island Line when the time was right. This decision was a very big step and was not done lightly, but it was felt to be the right thing to do to safeguard our future. Was it the right one?

In April 1995 our flagship locomotive *Calbourne* celebrated another anniversary, its 70th year on the Island, and happily to everyone's delight was back in service again after its overhaul. The Railway had a press day on 29th March to mark the re-launch of the 02 back into traffic.

But sadly it seems as one door opens a little, another one slams shut in your face; for just as *Calbourne* returned, W8 *Freshwater* had to be withdrawn with such serious boiler problems that it was thought to require a new one. Such is life! Another rolling stock crisis was on the cards when SR 15-ton goods brake No.55710 was withdrawn from service after structural defects were found with the braking gear and frames through corrosion.

One of the less glamourous sides to our business are the 'customer facilities', a polite way of talking about toilets. It is generally not a subject talked about openly, and I personally have not seen too much space given to the subject in the railway books I have read. Nevertheless we had been trading at Havenstreet since 1971 and had never thought that the toilet and sewerage systems would have to be upgraded as a priority. There was always a little voice in the wilderness saying that you should do something about the loos, but basically they kept being put down the list every year because something more important (we thought) had come up. The problem stemmed back to SR days, when the toilets had been built to cater for the relatively small numbers of travelling public and not the requirements of a major tourist attraction. They were old, shabby, a little smelly and drained into a cesspit that would, if over-filled discharge into a local stream.

Following severe criticism by the local water authority (do something or we prosecute) and also a stinging report by none other than the publisher Ian Allan, we at last grasped this particular large nettle. We built a new sewage treatment works at Havenstreet, which cost £40,000 and provided a full filtration plant to modern standards, and this allowed us to comply with new anti-pollution measures. The toilets themselves were totally up-graded and although still the same size and a little inadequate at some times, nevertheless looked very presentable. We have since provided additional facilities for disabled persons and with the opening of an extension to the refreshment room in 2005, we have added additional loos there. So having been forced into it a little, along with a reluctant parting of cash, we now have a reasonable standard of facilities for our visitors and hope to maintain that in the future.

As mentioned earlier, we had a goods brake crisis with all our brake vans in for repairs or awaiting the same. A plea to the Bluebell Railway resulted in a long-term loan of their 'Pillbox' SR 25-ton van No.55993 built in 1930, and this is a suitable place to acknowledge their kindness and support. The rest of 1995 was a little lacking in news, but we must have made a pretty good job of running the railway because we won the 1995 *Railway World* 'Independent Railway of the Year Award'. This yielded yet another plaque which was duly placed on the wall in the waiting room at Havenstreet station.

Meanwhile on the management side of the Railway, several changes were made at Board level and much talk was circulating about a visitor centre. This was the brainchild of several board members and although it was not a bad idea, a lot of ordinary staff and members thought the project too costly and a little ill-conceived. This, along with the very hush-hush progress on the franchise bid for Island Line, was causing some concern in certain quarters.

Above: *On the stock front, 25th July 1995 saw W11* Newport *return to service after overhaul, and a welcome sight it was too. Meanwhile, the boiler appeal for W8* Freshwater *was going well and we all hoped we would soon see scenes like this again.* Terry Hastings

In 1995 the Internet was a little known computer-thingy that expert whiz kids knew about and old codgers like me didn't. Fortunately, an expert among our number, James Watt (one of our drivers) got a small Isle of Wight Railway web-site up and running. This new quirky idea was, in my eyes along with lots of other eyes totally unnecessary, but the website created by James proved very popular and remained basically unchanged until 2000, giving visitors the information they required. In 2000, Tony and Carole Barry took over the website and totally revamped the format and it has since gone from strength to strength and is a super way of keeping up to date with what is going on at Havenstreet. The website is full of all sorts of information, ranging from when we are running, to what has been going on in the workshop and everything in-between; all the pages are clear, bright and easy to use. The website can be found at: - www.iwsteamrailway.co.uk

The 1995 season was in business parlance, a difficult trading year. This made the finances even tighter and all this with the added costs of the franchise bid draining hard-earned cash from the coffers. An appeal for a new boiler for W8 *Freshwater* was started and by the middle of 1996 it had reached £12,000, because all sorts of fund-raising ideas were being used to try and reach the target as soon as possible under the Directorship of Simon Futcher. The Railway at this time was busy putting together a Safety Case for the Health & Safety Executive.

Meanwhile the Railway's Board had decided that an exemption, the way most preserved railways had gone, was not for the Isle of Wight Steam Railway. We had an eye on the franchise of Island Line and with this in mind it was thought prudent to go for a full safety case approval by the Railway Inspectorate and this is what we did. Whether the decision was correct is something that has been debated ever since, but hindsight is a wonderful thing!

Sunday 28th January 1996 was the nearest to the date on which to celebrate the fact that, 25-years earlier, the railway had moved its collection of rolling stock and everything else of value from Newport to Havenstreet. An Anniversary Special was run using W24 *Calbourne*, complete with original headboard and a newer version displaying the words 'The Move 25-Years On'. Over 1,200 passengers enjoyed a free ride on the specials and there was a reunion of as many as possible of the people that had 'made it happen' back in 1971. The *Wight Report* for Summer 1996 contained a presentation about the Visitor Centre Project and associated works involved with moving the Mechanical Engineering department from the site they occupied to a new site on the Smallbrook side of the road bridge at Havenstreet in what is known as the 'Barn Field'.

On 1st September, Railway Chairman John Suggett outlined the story of the franchise bid, much of which had been confidential up to that point. It was to read much like this: "The Railway was informed that they had pre-qualified in late-June, and therefore were in the final selection process. The board met in July to discuss what action to take. Most preparatory work had been carried out in-house by necessity. The OPRAF timetable gave only six weeks to prepare the bid in full. Therefore it was decided to proceed in preparing the bid without actually committing to submit it."

It was known that some would be critical if a bid was made, whilst others would criticise if it were not, indeed, some would not forgive the Board if the opportunity was allowed to pass. It was a very difficult decision but eventually the 'ayes' on the right won it and the bid was made, the Board having felt it had acted with due diligence. A full bid was made in mid-August and was delivered to OPRAF on the 22nd. After a nervous wait of several weeks, it was announced in mid-September that Stagecoach was the preferred bidder and later in the month confirmed that they had won a five-year term, commencing on 13th October. The Board were clearly disappointed with the result and could only put a brave face on it and point out that some exercises in the bidding process would have long-term benefits to the Railway. All one can say is that a lot of money was spent on the bid (rightly or wrongly), but shortly after this time we had to take some pretty drastic action to make sure we continued in business.

On happier matters, although we had only part of the money required, a start had been made on construction of a new boiler for *Freshwater* by Israel Newton Limited of Bradford and would be ready in about six months. *Royal Engineer* was stopped for a major ten-year overhaul in the autumn of 1995 and required a complete re-tube. This had progressed very well and by early August 1996 it was again ready for action, this was just as well as *Calbourne* was suffering problems with leaking stays and requiring a boiler lift.

Much correspondence was received concerning the proposed visitor centre and the general consensus seemed to point to an overall dissatisfaction with the Board's stance on the issue, some even going to the extremes of questioning the grip on reality that some had. This situation was not helped by the increasing concerns about the dropping visitor numbers and financial problems. By Spring 1997 the reality of the situation was becoming clear. The Board members involved in the ill-fated visitor centre had resigned and the Railway had recognised that finances were in a parlous state, requiring bank loans to keep it afloat. The situation was not a happy one, but it was not impossible, steps had already been taken and although not yet satisfactory, the predicament had been stabilised. A local businessman, Hugh Boynton, was appointed as a Business Consultant to guide the Railway through 1997 and try to get us on an even keel with a structured financial plan.

On a more positive note, the tremendous efforts in fund raising for the Terrier boiler had netted a staggering £25,000 which meant that only a further £10,000 was required to meet our estimate costs. This was certainly more like the Railway that we had hoped for when the euphoria of the extension was at its height back in 1991. Meanwhile W11 was undergoing an overhaul with wheels having been sent away for profiling, but W24 had been inspected and found to need expensive work, so a decision was sadly taken to push it into the display siding until funds were available. So the 1997 season started on a more positive note with finance under control, and with the new Business Consultant having taken charge of expenditure we had formed a better management structure. Obviously our problems were not over but a better start to the season with more visitors than expected helped the situation immensely.

As a new Carriage & Wagon Workshop was being talked about as a major requirement for the future, a quantity of steel work was purchased from the former Island Bakery site in Binstead as the offer was too good to miss. Meanwhile, another long-running saga was unveiled in 1997 with regard to Ivatt 2-6-2 tank engines 41298 and 41313. It was reported that an agreement was close to being signed for the loan of these two locomotives from the Ivatt Trust, as negotiations about the possibility of these tanks coming to the Island had been carried out with trustees Roy Miller and Peter Clarke for a couple of years. It all sounded very positive and that the Ivatt's arrival was thought to be imminent. In fact it was not until 2006 that 41313 finally arrived on the Island, but its sister was still awaited at the time of writing. Another restored four-wheeler was almost ready for traffic, LBSCR Third No.2343, this was basically complete, but awaiting acceptance and inspection by the Railway Inspectorate. The hope was that it would not take too long!

Spring 1997 saw stalwart member George Wheeler step down from the job of Signal & Telegraph Supervisor. A full-time employee of BR, George had been involved with the Society right from the start and he had worked tirelessly over the years on many aspects of the Railway's development, but his particular favourite area was signalling. His ability to get installations together and working with minimum expenditure and basic facilities was amazing! He was almost always on his own and worked late into the evening with an old hurricane lamp providing light during winter months. Over the years several keen helpers joined George, among these were Cliff Munday and Ron Matten. Cliff was a time-served BR signalling technician and manager with a lifetime of experience on the Western Region, who after retirement had offered his services to help George. He proved an excellent volunteer, giving a lot of support and guidance when planning the re-signalling of Havenstreet for the opening of the extension, but he regretfully did not have a long retirement as he suffered a terminal illness and sadly passed away soon afterwards.

Ron Matten was to help George for many years with signalling matters, especially with telephone engineering. Ron had worked for the BBC and had a very good knowledge of electronics and communication systems and always managed to keep our aged telephone system working. Ron has also recently hung up his tool bag, but he continues to follow the railway's progress. When the S&T position became vacant, we were fortunate to secure the services of Viv Orchard, yet another time-served signal engineer who had recently retired from BR and moved to the Island. Viv had started his railway career in the signal works at Reading, and after many jobs around the railway finished his career with the Southern Region. He brought with him a wealth of experience and was instrumental in getting many S&T projects done during his time at the Railway.

Top Right: *Ivatt 2-6-2T 41298 seen at Quainton Road on 4th August 1997.* David Goulty

Bottom Right: *W11* Newport *shunts ex-LSWR road van No.56046 and is seen soon after its extensive overhaul.* IWR Collection

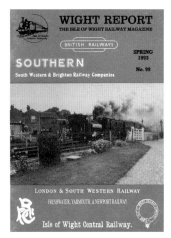

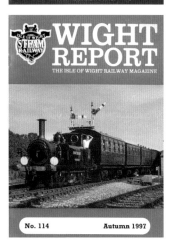

Left: *A selection of covers from the* Wight Report *magazine showing the way the publication has evolved over the years.*

Below: *A picture taken inside the signal box at Havenstreet, showing the frame dating from 1926, which was installed by the Southern Railway during the rebuilding of the station. The 16-lever frame is smaller than we now need, but with some clever design using selected signals we have managed to get a quart in a pint pot!* Jeff Layfield

Viv Orchard's eight years in charge of signalling saw many challenges, including several new signals commissioned, a complete re-signalling of Havenstreet to allow for bi-directional running through the loops and a re-locking of the Havenstreet signal box. Viv retired from the S&T Supervisor's job at the end of 2004, but he continues to assist the Railway as both a Director and volunteer.

As predicted Stagecoach Holdings took over the franchise for Island Line on 13th October 1997 and a staff of 44 were included in the franchise. Yet, strangely with the proximity of South West Trains (which is also a Stagecoach company), the Island Line operation was to be administered from their Lewes headquarters for bus operations. On our Railway, the Carriage & Wagon department finished a long overhaul on the LSWR road van No.56046 in July 1997. The brake van was in a very sorry state when it entered the works with many of the structural timbers so badly rotten that they needed complete replacement. The overhaul took a long time, but the finished result was worth every second; the restored vehicle looked a picture and the Railway again had a brake van to use on goods and engineering trains. This would allow us to return the loaned Bluebell brake van to its rightful home in Sussex later in the year. Meanwhile, the Health & Safety approval procedures having been rather prolonged were completed for the restored LBSCR four-wheel Third No.2343, allowing it to enter traffic on 3rd August 1997.

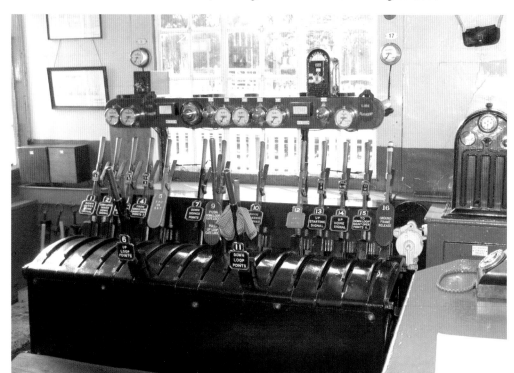

The *Wight Report* was, after 114 issues, to come to an end with the Autumn 1997 edition. It had been an extremely informative magazine under the editorship of Iain Whitlam and had kept the membership fully informed of the happenings on the Railway plus, thanks to the *Island Railway Notes and News* column compiled by Richard Newman, and details on the BR Island rail line, shipping services and old Island railway system including infrastructure, buildings and structures. The demanding nature of magazine production with deadlines, collection of material and editorial duties had got more and more difficult as the years rolled on, Iain had done a marvellous job but delays in producing the *Wight Report* had caused a little concern within the Railway management for a while.

The decision to produce a brand new format of magazine was an amicable one all round. Mike Smith in Croydon had started producing the newsletter in the early days with an old duplicator machine using an inked drum turned by handle, which produced a fairly legible sheet of printed matter if you were lucky. As times changed, more demands were made to the format, so that photographs, plans and suchlike could be included; George Wheeler and Richard Newman moved the journal to that next level.

Finally an A5 booklet format for the magazine evolved with Iain at the helm and the excellent publication was much loved by all. This format was to be used for many years but by 1997 some felt it to be a little dated, so a revamp was planned. In the interim period a basic newsletter type format was used until the planned colour A4 magazine was ready to be produced. The new journal was to be Island-based, and a full editorial team was formed to oversee everything including the printing, which was to be undertaken by a local firm. So Issue 114 was the last original format *Wight Report* and another part of the Railway passed into history, allowing Iain to retire his faithful typewriter.

The headline for the new interim newsletter in the Spring of 1998 was to read: "Planning permission refused for new Carriage & Wagon Workshop", which was not a very auspicious start! After a period of consolidation under the new management regime of Hugh Boynton, the Railway had started to look forward again with a new scheme for the area that had been earmarked for the ill-fated visitor centre. The need to create more space for both carriage and locomotive repair and restoration was of pressing concern. Up to now all this work had been carried out in the works that had been built alongside the platform at Havenstreet way back in the 1970s. Although a major step forward back then, it had become rather cramped as the locomotive and rolling stock numbers had grown over the years. This was seen as a serious problem, the answer was of course a purpose-built workshop that would separate the C&W from motive power and make much more room for engineering needs in general. An outline plan had been drawn up for the building, which we decided should be sited on the Goosefield.

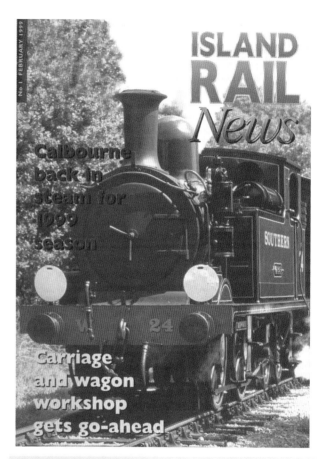

Top Right: *Issue No.1 of* Island Rail News *looked good and was received well.*

Bottom Right: *Brighton four-wheeler 2343, which won the Heritage Railway Association Special Commendation for 1999, looks superb in the sunshine at Havenstreet.* Brian Deegan

As stated this was turned down at a meeting of the Planning Authority in February 1998, however all was not lost, as the Authority was happy to reconsider the plans when certain issues had been resolved to do with the location and the type of building to be erected. So we went back to the drawing board and sharpened the pencil again!

A Happy Christmas was in store for *Freshwater* when the new boiler from Bradford was delivered in December 1997. It was craned straight into the frames and although there was a lot of fitting out to be done, the mechanical team were delighted with the standard of manufacture as all the critical dimensions were amazingly accurate, and thus reflected the skill and experience of the boilermakers. Work continued throughout the early months of 1998 allowing an early test steaming on 6th March, and although a few gremlins needed to be sorted out, it was ready for a return to service on 27th June. Invited guests, many of which were Railway supporters that had put a lot of money into the appeal, enjoyed a day of celebrations with *Freshwater* in Maunsell lined green livery pulling its first public train since the boiler troubles had forced its withdrawal. When the boiler had been condemned no-one had dared to presume when it would return, as the cost had seemed especially huge at a time when money was very tight. Yet, the enthusiasm and generosity of both members and the general public had been staggering, allowing us to return it to traffic so quickly.

In October 1997 a small defect with the Havenstreet signal box locking turned out to be a huge problem, after an independent locking inspector confirmed that the mechanism was life-expired and had to be completely renewed. Having to re-lock the signal box gave us an opportunity to change some aspects of the old signalling to a more suitable system in tune with our present operations. Charles Hudson, a very experienced former BR locking engineer (working for amongst others, the Bluebell Railway) very kindly drew up plans.

With work required on new signals, point control, re-wiring and the locking, the project amounted to a huge workload. Our Civil Engineering staff completed almost all the locking and associated engineering work in-house, with our mechanical workshop providing much-needed help with welding and precision work. The project took a lot longer than first envisaged and it was not completed until June 1998. Dave Marriot, a Certified Tester, carried out a final independent test on 21st June and all other work was done soon after. This allowed the signal box to be brought back into normal use just in time for the high summer, much to the delight of the operating department who could put the point clips and flags back in the emergency box.

February 1999 saw the first issue of *Island Rail News* being published in colour and full of big bold pictures. The news it contained was good as well, as *Calbourne* was to be repaired and hopefully back in steam again for the forthcoming season. Furthermore, after re-applying for planning permission for the Carriage & Wagon workshop we had finally got the go-ahead. W24 had undergone a full survey and it had been decided to use a new procedure for copper welding. This would give the firebox an extra lease of life rather than having to renew the plates as previously thought. The hope was that the repairs would last until the next ten-year overhaul due in 2004.

The Carriage & Wagon workshop appeal had also got off to a good start, with a sum of £11,000 already in the coffers. This had started more or less after the completion of the Terrier boiler appeal. It was thought a sum of £50,000 would be required, which together with hoped-for money from the Rural Development Programme and a Lottery Grant would be sufficient to meet the bill for the new building. The planning permission had been granted on the understanding that the structure must be built using brickwork, so as to blend in with other buildings around the site, however this had substantially increased the cost.

On the rolling stock front we won a commendation for a four-wheeler in The Heritage Railway Association's annual coach competition. The newest recruit to our growing fleet had been Billinton-designed LBSCR No.2343, following the protracted commissioning by the inspectorate reported earlier. The Heritage Railway Association held its Spring meeting at Birmingham and Jim Loe accepted the award on behalf of the Railway. Thanks to the C&W boys, the trophy cabinet was groaning under the weight. The next four-wheel coach body was then set on its underframe, this being LCDR Third Class No.2515; but there's no rest for the wicked!

A surprise report appeared in *IRN* No.2, announcing the proposed visit of a 'foreign' locomotive to take part in a gala weekend. This was to be LBSCR E4 Class, 473 (BR 32473) *Birch Grove*. Negotiations with the Bluebell Railway were in hand and a proposed date in August was planned for the visit. This would be the first time a visiting engine had ever been on the Isle of Wight Railway and this was seen as a bit of an experiment. This was entirely appropriate, as in 1947 the Southern Railway had done a similar thing with another of the very same E4 Class when No.2510 had arrived on the Island for testing. The plan was to try the locomotive on large push-pull trains on the Ryde-Ventnor line, but Island clearances were very tight and after clipping several platform edges, it spent most of its time either on the Newport-Sandown line or dumped at the back of Newport depot. Consequently No.2510 did not find favour on the Island and was returned to the mainland to resume its career there!

The work on *Calbourne* was progressing nicely, with firebox welding completed in January 1999. By March the hydraulic test on the boiler was carried out and it passed with flying colours so a steam test was carried out on 25th May, and the very next day it was put back into service on passenger trains. This was the first time the O2 had been in service since 12th September 1996!

The complete plan of the proposed Carriage & Wagon workshop was available by mid-1999 and with it came lots and lots of work; for example, the Goosefield sidings complex would need to be altered completely. This was quite an undertaking as all the sidings had previously been put in and built up with chalk in-fill to make a safe area to walk around. This entire fill would need to be dug out, a lot by hand, before the sidings could be moved or dismantled. A start was made in July on this work and the progress was very good, just as well because a siding was required by 13th August to allow for the delivery of a 57-ton monster, namely *Birch Grove*.

Top & Middle Right: *One carriage rolls out and another gets rolled in, as we can see when 2515 is lifted and made ready to enter the works.* Brian Deegan

Bottom Right: *Work starts on alterations in the Goosefield ready to build the new Carriage & Wagon Workshop.* Brian Deegan

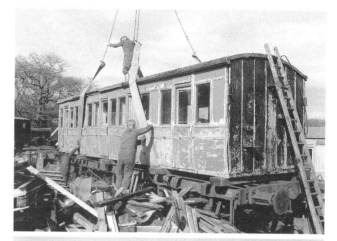

Meanwhile the fund-raising department was going great guns, as the C&W Workshop Fund had now passed £14,000. This was tempered with the news that the current cost for the building was now around £300,000, most of which would, it was hoped be met by a Heritage Lottery Fund Grant of £225,000 and a grant from the IW Rural Development Programme of £30,000. The grant applications were expected to be made in 2000 with a decision expected about six months later. If the grant application was unsuccessful it would mean going back to the drawing board! Work commenced on the restoration of four-wheel coach No.2515 with plans to convert two compartments into areas suitable for wheelchairs. This would be done very sympathetically, keeping the outside panelling as original as possible, but allowing for double door access with ramps to facilitate the easy loading and unloading of wheelchair-bound passengers.

In August, as promised, on the back of John Antell's low-loader came a big brown locomotive called *Birch Grove*. After a few checks and some clearance testing that went well, No.473 entered traffic and became the star attraction at the rail gala held over the weekend of the 21st-22nd August. The Railway produced a great weekend with all three Island engines in use along with our visitor. Crowds enjoyed regular double-heading on passenger trains and a demonstration goods train. When the Bluebell kindly allowed us to keep *Birch Grove* for a little longer, she stayed and helped out over the 25th anniversary of the steam show weekend as well. The Steam Show was first established in 1975 and was held to commemorate the centenary of the Ryde-Newport Railway. This was a two day event with three traction engines in steam, one catering outlet (a paste table and tablecloth), and saw over 3,000 people in attendance.

The 25th Island Steam Show in 1999 was a massive four-day event, and had 25 traction engines in steam; nine separate catering outlets, 11,000 visitors and revenue of approximately £80,000. The show, being an annual event, is the biggest single undertaking the Railway has in the course of the year. A whole team of volunteers plan, build, man and dismantle the show over a two-week period. Many of these stalwarts have done this for years and it is not unusual for some to use a full fortnight's holiday entitlement from their usual employment to come and work really hard to present a super steam extravaganza. This is the sort of commitment that makes the Railway what it is and our volunteers so special.

The *Island Rail News* gamble paid off as we won a trophy for 'Most Improved Magazine' from the Heritage Railway Association, and also came third in 'Best Magazine' category. The decision to enlarge *Wight Report* from A5 to A4 and change the name had been both controversial and had many members up in arms, but the new magazine's popularity and award-winning format had shown that the change was for the best in the long term.

COMINGS AND GOINGS

As the century drew to a close, it was again a time of change. Over on Island Line both the 03 shunter's were sold and left the Island. First, 03079 was collected from Sandown and transported to Murton, near York, for operation on the Derwent Valley Railway. This was entirely appropriate, as this particular engine had been allocated in the North East before its transfer to the Island in 1984. The other (03179, in NSE livery) ran under its own power from Ryde St Johns Road to Sandown after services finished on 31st May 1998 and departed two weeks later for Hornsey, North London, where it started work for West Anglia Great Northern on shunting duties at the EMU depot. At the time, this was the only Class 03 shunter still in use on the former BR system.

Above: *The return of* Calbourne *came after the firebox welding, which we hoped would give us a few more years of usage before the major overhaul due in 2004, sadly it was not to be.* Brian Deegan

Another old railwayman, Joe Snellgrove, regrettably passed away in July 1998. He had been a boilersmith in Ryde Works for many years, and had helped the fledgling Railway by putting in considerable time at Havenstreet to assist with the re-tubing of *Calbourne*. He passed on his many and valuable skills, gained in a lifetime of looking after boilers on the Island steam locomotives, to the Railway volunteers and workshop staff. His memory will live on as a wooden bench seat was dedicated to Joe and this was sited in the station gardens at Havenstreet.

The new management regime had no doubt been a success, the finances were going in the right direction and bank loans were fortunately a thing of the past. Hugh Boynton, the Business Consultant, had done a wonderful job in steering the Railway away from the rocks of financial ruin and had turned the ship onto the steady course of living within its means. All this work had cemented his relationship with the Board and managers, thus it was no surprise when he was offered, and accepted, the job of Chief Executive/General Manager. He was appointed to this position in November 1999 and as stated by the Board members "this simply reflects what Hugh has effectively been doing for the past three years."

As 1999 drew to a close we ran the 'last IWR train of the 20th Century' on 31st December, which was hauled by *Royal Engineer* with Ken West at the controls. The train was given the 'right away' by 84-year old May Joyce, the first (and only) lady guard on the Isle of Wight system before preservation. She had worked as a passenger guard during the war years and on our special train she entertained fellow travellers with tales of how it used to be.

The Isle of Wight Steam Railway had always been a little different to other mainland railways. Our unique position, overseas as it were, had precluded us from doing many of the things other preserved lines were doing such as locomotive swaps and special events. The costs of transporting rolling stock to and from the Island had always been high and this also held true for getting materials or services across too. In the early days of the society a large load on one of the old car ferries would almost mean a boat to ourselves, as the size would mean that nothing much else would fit on the ferry.

Thankfully car ferries have grown in size as services got both busier and more regular. Nowadays the ferries run 24-hours a day with a capacity that is quite staggering. Our friendship with Wightlink and Red Funnel ferries has helped enormously with costs, as sponsorship and discounts from both organisations have helped us to put on more and more events that require a large movement of vehicles from the mainland. Thus we at last agreed to put on a 'Day Out with Thomas' event. We were probably the last sizeable preserved railway to start 'Thomas' events, although we had looked at it years earlier before coming to the conclusion that the costs would outweigh the benefits. Gladly this was now no longer the case and we negotiated a deal for a weekend taking in the 7th to 10th July with 'Thomas' coming to us from the Mid Hants line.

Top Right: *Easing* Birch Grove *down from the low-loader transport onto the newly laid loading/unloading road that leads from the car park into the Goosefield at Havenstreet on 13th August 1999.* Di Akers

Middle Right: *The 25th Island Steam Show, with Fowlers Showman's road locomotive* Lion *lit up in the evening darkness.* Pete Snashall

Bottom Right: *The 'galloping horses' roundabout pictured during the Steam show weekend in 1999.* Pete Snashall

Above: *A fine shot of LBSCR E4 Class No.473* Birch Grove, *during its first visit to the Isle of Wight Railway in August 1999. The headboard can be taken either way –* The Tourist *was the named through service from Ventnor to Freshwater mentioned earlier, but I imagine some wag in the locomotive department thought it appropriate on this engine, as it was exactly the right description!* Brian Deegan

Left: *Maybe not every enthusiast's favourite kind of event, but making money is not negotiable these days. 'Thomas', the Fat Controller and Mrs Kyndley entertain the kids on Havenstreet platform at our first 'Day out with* Thomas' *event in 2000. Using our own Class 03 diesel as 'Mavis' and an assortment of coaches and troublesome trucks the event was an immediate success. The popularity of the Reverend Awdrey's books and characters has never waned, in fact the television and spin-off merchandise had increased the appeal so much that we had a bumper weekend. As with all things, we tried this event as a toe in the water, and the success was instant!* Patrick Eden

Ever since that first '*Thomas*' event in 2000, it has become a regular feature of the summer season and the Island of Wight is transformed into the Island of Sodor for four days, '*Thomas*' always coming over to meet his friends at the Railway and do battle with a few troublesome trucks.

Island Line trains were re-branded during 2000 with a local theme of dinosaurs, although this was not thought to have any reference to the age of the stock! Actually, the Isle of Wight had always been famous for its hidden treasure of fossils along the coastal cliffs, so much so that a farm had been converted into a dinosaur museum and a purpose-built display of fossils and dinosaur-related models was planned for Sandown sea-front. Therefore, when the management of Stagecoach were looking for a suitable livery for Island Line trains to take over from the ageing Network SouthEast livery, they used a colourful and complicated mix of paint and vinyl decals depicting the prehistoric creatures. The first two units to be treated were 004 and 006. The remainder of the fleet were changed later with the exception of 007, which was repainted in original London Transport livery.

Fortunately, *Royal Engineer* and Barclay diesel shunter No.235, which had come on loan from the National Army Museum (NAM) were to stay on the Island for a longer period than first envisaged. The original loan agreement would have expired in 2002, but a new loan period was arranged and this would be considerably longer, certainly giving us another five-years at least. Whilst '*Thomas*' was resident at Havenstreet, the chance was taken to use its transporter and move some rolling stock recently purchased from Sandown and Eastleigh.

Island Line having decided that track maintenance would no longer require the services of a dedicated fleet of rolling stock offered the lot in one go during the summer of 2000. We agreed to purchase some of the wagons, and the others went to homes on the mainland. We received DS70000, informally named *Britannia* (because of the number); this was a bogie rail carrier that carried two Geismar rail cranes. We also acquired two match wagons, DB452219 and DB453255, that worked with the *Britannia*.

We also received DE263276, a 25-ton ex-LNER Lowmac, DB992730, a 24-ton Dogfish ballast hopper wagon and DS55724, a SR 15-ton Goods Brake Van that was to the same design as 55710, which was already with us. From Eastleigh we received the following, S210 (Internal user No.083618) a SR Bogie Van B and DS70239, a SR CCT converted to a Staff & Tool Van. The last two vehicles were purchased to provide underframes and spares but the vehicles from Sandown were all obtained for use on engineering duties and were to be overhauled with a view to continued use.

Top Right: *May Joyce, the Island's World War II lady passenger Guard, gives the 'right away' to the last train of the century, which was hauled by* Royal Engineer *with the veteran drive Ken West at the controls*. Di Akers

Bottom Right: Freshwater *is seen at Horsted Keynes whilst visiting the Bluebell Railway during the winter of 2000/01*. IWR Collection

Top & Middle Left: *The new livery applied to the ex-LT class 483 units at Ryde Pier Head (top) and St John's Road.* IWR Collection

Bottom Left: *Receiving the Independent Railway of the Year Award is IWR Chairman, John Suggett (middle) from Sir Alastair Morton (left) and Ian Allan (right), at the ceremony in London during December 2000.* IWR Collection

So we came to the end of another satisfactory season, for although visitor numbers to the Island were poor, 2000 had been a very successful year. Our new events had brought lots more interest from the public and enthusiasts alike, thus making us much more money. The Railway was really back on its feet after the rocky time previously reported, but none of us dreamt that the *Railway World* 'Independent Railway of the Year Award' would again come to the Isle of Wight, but it did! We won this prestigious award for, I quote, "being a superb reproduction of the Island's railways in the pre-war and immediate post-war days." The Railway Chairman, John Suggett, travelled to London to collect the award from Sir Alastair Morton, then Chairman of the Strategic Rail Authority, and Ian Allan.

This was the third time the Railway had won this award, which we believed was a record. It was a real feather in our cap, as the judgement criteria was very demanding and the competition very strong, but even so we obviously came through all the tests very well to secure votes from the judges. The Railway having been put on the 'straight and narrow' financially was looking to the future, and a new extension to the refreshment room was underway. This was intended to be finished ready for the 2001 season, and a planned purchase of a field adjacent to the Havenstreet site for additional siding space was being given serious consideration. The C&W workshop appeal was progressing well with £14,000 now bulging the bank balance somewhat.

After *Birch Grove* had visited the Island during the summer of 2000, it was part of the deal that our two Terriers would visit the Bluebell Railway during the winter and have a bit of a gala with their mates *Stepney* and *Fenchurch*. Both *Newport* and *Freshwater* made the trip to Sussex and obviously so enjoyed their time there that they didn't return to the Island until Spring 2001.

After a sojourn of many years our 0-4-0ST *Invincible* was almost ready after a lengthy overhaul. As the Railway was now much longer, the little Hawthorn Leslie was a bit limited on what it could do on passenger trains. The locomotive was certainly strong enough and had plenty of puff, but only with a small train; even then its limited coal and water capacity made it difficult unless it was operated on a special timetable to allow for regular servicing stops. Nevertheless the membership and staff were fond of old *Invincible*, as it really did keep the Railway alive back in the early 1970s when we had no other working locomotives. We owed the locomotive a lot, so it was nice to see it coming along, a hydraulic test was passed and when finished it was painted in Woolwich Arsenal maroon livery. *Invincible* even had a brief holiday on the Bluebell Railway helping out at a '*Thomas*' event, by way of a thank you!

Film-makers are strange folk, often with very strange requests and a pocket full of £10 notes to make that request a reality. So it was when we received an approach from Paramount Pictures to see if we would allow use of three of our bogie coaches. This didn't seem too much to ask, not really a problem, when would you like them and for how long? "Oh", they replied "only three days filming but not on the Island; we want them at Loughborough, on the Great Central line!" Now would you do that if you were making a film, even if you wanted to portray an accurate railway scene! But that's what they wanted and not known to turn down a pocket full of money the three coaches, 2416, 6349 and 4145 duly went on a 170-mile drive up the motorway so that Nicole Kidman and Meryl Streep could do what the director wanted for three days and then they came back down the motorway. The film, by the way was called *The Hours*; I must admit I have never seen it, but if you do look out for the train scenes, you must not blink because it cost them an awful lot of money!

Now, because our Terriers had such a good time down in the depths of Sussex during the Winter, we felt it only right and proper to return the compliment and have the Bluebell Terriers over to our place for a little bash. Therefore over the period of 21st to 29th July 2001, we had four of those lovely little engines operating on the Isle of Wight. This was not a first on the Island, as the Southern Railway had managed a few more than that between the wars, but it certainly was a first in the preservation era. Both *Fenchurch* and *Stepney* were very welcome additions to the fleet and created lots of interest from the enthusiasts for the gala period. No.672 *Fenchurch* was dual-braked, which was a real bonus as most mainland-based locomotives are only vacuum braked for compatibility with the rolling stock so designed. The Island system of air-braked stock had been rare on the mainland during the steam era, thus making life difficult with locomotive exchanges and such like.

Strangely the modern railway braking systems have gone full circle and now use air-brakes as standard, vacuum having been largely superseded on all but preserved lines. *Fenchurch* was thus allowed to pull passenger trains on its own having the facility to work the continuous brake throughout the train, *Stepney* on the other hand was only vacuum-braked so could only work goods trains or work double-headed on passenger trains with an air fitted locomotive. This did not detract from the event though and all concerned thought it to be the best event yet on the IWR.

Marion Hunnisett was (and still is) a long-serving member of the volunteer force, having been through thick and thin with the Railway, from early days at Newport to her valuable work these days keeping gardens and the woodland walk at Havenstreet in perfect condition. She delights in bringing a deal of humour into it with her unique collection of characters and artefacts made from all sorts of scrap collected from the site. Her ability to write funny little items to accompany these scrap sculptures makes the whole thing very quirky and charming for the public when they are wandering round. Marion has also set her reminiscences of Wight Locomotive Society days at Newport down in articles in the *Island Rail News*, which are a super read. Many of the stories are very humourous and involve many of the volunteer antics of the early preservation days and of the characters that prevailed at that time, some of whom are still around, I may add! Tales of odd types living in the station house at Newport, of courting couples using our beloved carriage stock for nocturnal liaisons, of officious BR staff and scrapmen; it is all there and really should form the companion volume to this, maybe I can persuade her one day!

The Board had agreed to purchase the field mentioned earlier to allow for a new siding complex, to be called 'Griffin's Sidings' after Mr. Griffin, the farmer from whom the land was purchased. To gain access to the field a tight curve would be required leading from the existing head-shunt to the west of the station. Pointwork to fit in the very limited area available was proving difficult to find. Roger Silsbury, a long-standing volunteer and full time Captain for the pilot service, had espied a couple of spare double slip points within the Southampton Docks rail complex. After a chat with Associated British Ports (ABP) he had found out they would be happy for us to remove them and install plain track in the gap if we wanted them. The weekend of the 8-9th September 2001 was chosen and a large team of PW staff and volunteers went 'overseas' to dismantle the slips and load them on to lorries for transport to Havenstreet. We had been led to believe that time was not a problem as trains were not scheduled to use the docks on Saturdays and Sundays. Wrong! We were informed on the Thursday before the job that two trains were in on Saturday, one early morning and one at teatime. We needed to work fast, but our workforce was brilliant and although we held the English Welsh & Scottish gypsum train up for about 30 minutes, we got the job done and we were the proud owners of two double slips.

Below: *If you think that this does not look like an Isle of Wight station, you would be right. However, it is Island stock we see 'on location' whilst three IoW coaches pause during the filming by the platform at Loughborough Central coupled to a coach of an uncertain pedigree!* Len Pullinger

A Duke, The Queen and A Double Slip-up

A proud moment in our history came on 20th August 2001, when we paid host to a visit from HRH the Duke of Edinburgh. The Duke, who was escorted around the Railway by the Chairman and Chief Executive/General Manager showed a great deal of interest in our operations and history. After being presented with a plaque, the Duke proceeded to the locomotive W24 *Calbourne* for a footplate trip to Wootton and back with driver Ken West. The fireman brought out a pristine shovel especially for use that day, one that had only ever previously been used on the visit of HRH Lord Mountbatten in 1976. When would it be needed again we wondered?

Griffin's Sidings were to take shape rapidly during 2001 and by October the bulk of the track work was in situ, the two slips from Southampton had been made into one good one and was almost ready to be moved into position in the head-shunt. We had also received good news on the C&W Workshop front, with approval for Stage One of Heritage, Lottery Funding granted in September. This meant that the Trustees had approved the overall project, thereby allowing it to progress to the next stage.

Above: Freshwater *gets up close and friendly to a long-lost fellow Terrier, No.55* Stepney *in the yard at Havenstreet after a loan arrangement was agreed with the Bluebell Railway for their use during the 2001 rail gala.* Pete Snashall

This was by no means a cast-iron guarantee that we would get funding, much more information on the project would need to be compiled for the lottery trustees, before a final decision would be made; but it was good news nonetheless. The C&W Workshop fund raising efforts were still doing well, with the figure then reaching a staggering £62,000.

On the locomotive front, *Royal Engineer* had suffered a premature failure of its boiler tubes, despite their being only five-years-old. The decision was made to totally re-tube after investigations found that many tubes were very thin. The work was carried out quite swiftly and thankfully no major problems were encountered. The locomotive was tested and then steamed in November, returning to service over the Santa Special period. Brighton Terrier *Newport* was inspected and given a further 12-month's ticket, but would then require a full ten-year overhaul, with extensive repairs forecast.

In case you had forgotten about our Barclay tank *Ajax*, it is worth pointing out that this was still in the workshops and being worked when possible. No priority had been given to this locomotive, but work had progressed slowly until the time came to remove the boiler. It was then decided to send it away for work at Bartlett Engineering of Tenby, South Wales and subsequently left the Railway on 5th January 2002.

Prior to its departure *Invincible* had been test steamed in December 2001 and after a bit of fine-tuning was found to be in good order. Subsequently she was used on several days of Santa Specials for test steaming, but this didn't go to waste as it was attached to the Santa train carriages to warm their heating systems through. Several items remained to be done including work on the Westinghouse brake pump but nonetheless things were progressing well and W37 would be available for traffic in 2002. Back to the Griffin's Sidings, work carried on during the winter of 2001/02 and we were 'dead chuffed' in February 2002, when 03 diesel shunter D2059 with ex-LT ballast hoppers ground their way round the curve to dump the stone on the newly laid track. The sidings would be pressed into use almost immediately with stock having to move from the Goosefield ready for the proposed C&W Workshop earthworks.

Paradoxically, soon after we had finished ballasting the sidings we received a request from Island Line (they of the ethos that no engineering train is required) asking if they could borrow our shunter and ballast wagons. How could we refuse, after a bit of refresher training for their drivers, they borrowed the train for a 'weekend possession' in March, when a large amount of relaying and re-ballasting was carried out in the Sandown-Lake area.

Celebrations were in order in May 2002, as we had a 'bit of a do' to officially open Griffin's Sidings. We invited many guests most of whom had assisted the project, but the actual opening of the Sidings was carried out by the principle guest of honour, Mr Andrew Kent, Port Director, ABP Southampton. The ceremony involved Mr. Kent blowing a whistle and waving a green flag to signal 'right away' to the Driver of W37 *Invincible* to break through the tape and enter the siding complex. After the proceedings had finished, the guests were invited onto a special train of four-wheelers pulled by *Invincible* for a round trip on the whole line returning to the refreshment room for a cake cutting exercise and buffet.

Just a month later even more celebrations were in order when news arrived from the Heritage Lottery Fund that we had been successful in our bid. We were to receive a sum totalling £489,000 for part of the cost of the new workshop building with the residue to go towards the restoration programme for the following ten-years after completion.

Top Right: *Marion Hunnisett's teddy bears,* Stroudley *and* Billinton *have been around for 30-years, raising funds for the railway.* IWR Collection

Bottom Right: *Here EWS 66140 waits at the red banner, whilst the finishing touches are put to the plain line we have just laid in at Southampton Docks. Timing is everything so they say!* Tony Barry

Above: *Fenchurch makes a fine sight pulling out of Havenstreet for Smallbrook Junction with a train of four wheel coaches in July 2001.* IWR Collection

This future work involved restoring a number of vehicles, all of which were highlighted by us as the most deserving for either historical or commercial reasons. We had also secured a grant of £45,000 from the Rural Development Programme so it was celebrations all round.

Yet we felt we were to see the end of an era when *Calbourne* was withdrawn from service on Friday 9th August 2002. At the controls on the last day was driver Ken West who, at 73-years of age, doubted that he would still be driving when *Calbourne* would be ready to take to the rails again following the extensive repairs needed. Ken was right as four years down the road, *Calbourne* is still awaiting a return to service and Ken has now retired from regular driving turns at Havenstreet; but you never know! The 02 had secured a Lottery grant for the boiler work required and at the date of writing the work was underway with a view to completion in 2007/8. Ken is still very well and if everything goes according to plan we may still see the 'Man and his Steed' together again.

Work on clearing the Goosefield site ready for the start of the building work was commenced in October, but before we could start there were years of accumulated junk, underframes, coach bodies and more junk that had to be moved to other areas or the skip. Once this was done, more siding dismantling was needed to allow free access by the builders to dig for footings.

The reluctant Barclay tank *Ajax* was re-united with its boiler in October after its overhaul in Wales. The plan was to speed up the overhaul of this locomotive to cover for *Calbourne*'s early withdrawal. It was hoped to get the work finished in time for the 2003 season, but serious engineering problems had already made that look an impossible feat because we also needed to use staff to clear the Goosefield and the associated works involved with the new C&W Workshop.

So another season finished and an encouraging report was made by our Commercial Department about the year's takings. The advent of more special events and evening services had certainly seen our cash-flow improve and the coach traffic that had been generated over the previous few years had also seen a significant increase in revenue. The continuing trend was on the up with a tidy sum safely deposited in the bank.

The locomotive situation was not quite so happy, with *Royal Engineer* again being our only large engine for the heavier summer trains in 2003. Once again we turned to our good friends at Sheffield Park, Sussex and asked if we could hire *Birch Grove* for a few weeks. Thankfully for us they agreed and an arrangement was sorted out for No.473 to come to the Island in July and return to the Bluebell in September.

Over on Island Line the 'missing train' rejoined the fleet of 483 class units when 007 (licensed to thrill) came out of works resplendent in London Transport's 1938 livery. It certainly looked very impressive and stood out markedly from its five sister units that all carried the dinosaur paint scheme. With the 2003 season approaching we were informed of yet another award for a new four-wheeler. Having started the ball rolling all those years ago with NLR No.46, we didn't think that we could keep on winning awards for our efforts, but we had. As mentioned earlier 2515 was to be a special coach as we were working to provide a disabled area within the carriage but without affecting the outside appearance of the coach.

Our restoration team had done a magnificent job on this coach and the Heritage Railway Association thought so too. Their citation was to read: - "A stunning restoration which looks absolutely in place in its IoW setting. The restoration has included sympathetic modifications to accommodate wheelchairs utilising the former Guard's and adjacent compartments. The whole vehicle is superb and the 'disabled access' just doesn't show at all".

This project was again overseen by volunteer Pete Jardine (Special Projects Supervisor) and staff member John James (C&W Supervisor) who, along with a marvellous team of dedicated volunteers, were responsible for turning out this wonderful example of preserved rolling stock. The coach was to enter service in the 2003 season having had a history reading like this: - Built for the LCDR in 1894 as a six-wheeler at Longhedge Works (Stewarts Lane), London as a second class four-compartment brake coach, it was later downgraded to third class, and in 1916 it had the middle wheels and Guard's duckets removed. Selected for use on the Island in 1929, the Guard's compartment was replaced with a fifth third class one and sent to the Island in 1930.

Top Right: *HRH The Duke of Edinburgh gets a warm welcome from the children who were already aboard the train at Havenstreet. The visit continued the links that the Royal family have had since Queen Victoria visited here in the 19th Century.* Patrick Eden

Middle Right: *IWR's Class 03 shunter D2059 and ballast wagons in Sandown PW yard ready for action, after they had been 'hired' by Island Line to undertake engineering work on the electrified 'main line'.* Len Pullinger

Bottom Right: Here we see *W37* Invincible *as it breaks the official tape to open Griffin's Sidings. The double slip, acquired from Southampton, had been worked on for several months bringing it up to the standard we required.* Brian Deegan

Top Left: *Pete Jardine fixes luggage rack netting in LCDR coach No.2515.* Tony Barry

Middle Left: *A view of LCDR No.2515 showing the new door arrangement that would allow wheelchair access. With the doors closed the exterior of the vehicle is virtually unchanged.* Tony Barry

Bottom Left: *Bomb (lightning) damage at Wootton.* Tony Kerley

Withdrawn in 1937, the body of No.2515 was bought by the Fry family of Newport who sited it at Brambles Chine, Colwell, as a summer chalet, appropriately named 'Sunny Sidings'. It was donated to the WLS and moved to Havenstreet in 1981. Restoration commenced in 1999, when it was mounted on modified PMV frame No.S1497S. The next four-wheel coach body to be readied for work was LCDR No.6378 that would be put atop ex-PMV frame No.S1783S, which was already in the works for shortening.

The new C&W Workshop scheme was progressing well; the groundwork was done during the winter of 2002 and by spring 2003 the steelwork was up and a start made on the roofing. The rails had been delivered and sited on the concrete bases ready for fixing, and it all looked very good. Another new special event was planned for 2003 season. Our shop manager, Ted Green, was a particular enthusiast of 1940s wartime events and had finally got the go-ahead to try a wartime themed event at Havenstreet. It was another case of us being a little late in staging this type of event, as most large preserved lines had got similar events already running. However, better late than never, so we set aside the weekend of the 21st to 22nd June. A good deal of work went into getting the station and surrounds looking right for a wartime period and the 1940s society re-enactors with their wealth of uniforms and period clothing, the military vehicles and such like made a very convincing effect. We even had a bombing attack, which knocked out part of the line! Well not exactly but it was very close, the Saturday was normal with nothing untoward until the evening when storms brewed up from the south.

After thundery rumbles all night, the morning was still very stormy and I awoke to a tremendously loud clap of thunder above my home in Godshill, about five-miles from Havenstreet. Thinking nothing of it, I went to work at the usual time and prepared for another day in track maintenance, which is my forte. However, an urgent message was then received, "could I go to Wootton, because a tree had fallen down."

Getting a few tools together I drove round to the station at Wootton and was confronted with a huge pine tree completely smashed to pieces by a direct lightning strike laying across the platform and engine release head-shunt. My little bow saw was clearly not going to make any impact on this, and I would have been there till the next 1940s weekend dealing with that. A quick return to HQ ensued and luckily a local tree specialist was happy to turn out and help. The next few hours were spent cutting, pulling and disposing of many tons of pine. A bolt of lightning had travelled down the tree and literally blown it apart, the smell of sulphur and pine was quite strong when we started work.

The volunteer team as usual rallied round very quickly and many trailer loads of wood and foliage were sent to Havenstreet as we cleared the platform and track. Later a train was sent up to collect the remains and clear up the damaged fencing etc. A massive effort by everyone saw the line re-open for passenger traffic in time for the last trip of the day, so as in days of war the 'enemy action' was only to disrupt services for a short while.

The C&W workshop building work had been completed in the Goosefield by July, but although the brickwork outside looked super, much work was required inside. The promised loan of *Birch Grove* was fulfilled on 17th July, and once again this graceful locomotive ran services with our own engines until the end of the peak season in early September.

Every preservation group has its characters and our Railway is no exception, and just occasionally one of these characters makes such an impact that if they suddenly disappear everyone is deeply shocked and saddened. This happened to us on 30th July 2003 when one of our best-loved volunteers died suddenly at work of a heart attack. Chris (Andy) Anderton was a super chap, born in 1946 in Suffolk. He had been involved with the Railway since 1970 and passed out as a driver in 1977. He was always recognised for his competence and professionalism when driving and also for the brisk style he employed. He was known for his sense of humour and sense of fun, a good example being when he fitted a South African style hooter to our little saddle tank *Invincible*. When the Chairman, John Suggett asked why it was fitted, "To keep elephants off the track" he said. "But we haven't got any elephants on the line" answered John, "Well" said Andy, "that just shows how effective it is doesn't it." We were all stunned when Andy died at only 57; he had worked for Island Line at Ryde Works for several years, keeping the electric trains in good order and really enjoyed his employment there. In his spare time he was either with his wife and family or at Havenstreet driving trains or his vintage tractors. He was and still is, sadly missed.

Back to happier matters, a concerted effort through the Winter of 2003-4 saw the fitting out of the C&W workshop finished and the rail connection into the shed completed. We had a lot of PW work to do, as the new layout required that all the points in the Goosefield had to be moved from the workshop by about 30 feet. That doesn't sound much but when you have to do most work by hand it is quite an undertaking. Still we managed to get it all done within a reasonable time scale and got the first connection (No.1 road) finished in December 2003 and No.2 road in January 2004. The first vehicles in the new workshop were to be the underframe for the next four-wheeler No.6378 and restored coach 2515, which came in for minor work.

Preliminary investigations into the state of *Calbourne*'s boiler in early 2004 had found that very major repairs were necessary. It was thought that it might be worth trying for a Lottery Grant, and although we had only just got one for the C&W Workshop, it was quite possible that the 02 would be deemed another excellent cause. Meanwhile as a proportion of the cost would always need to be found by the Railway, it was felt that a boiler appeal should be started.

Above: *The Home Guard took 'em young; here an apprehensive youth guards a station seat.* Tony Kerley

Do you remember the story of the shovel that only comes out for royalty? Well we had to dust it off again in 2004, and this time it had to be shone up to the maximum. Her Majesty the Queen was to visit the Island for various engagements and we were honoured to find that an official opening of the Carriage & Wagon Workshop would be one of these. Lots of work went into getting all the arrangements in place before the appointed day.

The itinerary for the visit by Her Majesty Queen Elizabeth II; was as follows, Driver Bob Millard, Fireman David Smith and Guard Kim Chalkley got the Royal Train ready at Havenstreet with W8 *Freshwater* and proceeded to Wootton. After running around and moving the train to the exact spot, all was ready for the arrival of the Queen. The Royal car swept into the car park and with cheers ringing around from the waiting crowds, the Queen was introduced to John Suggett and Hugh Boynton by the Lord Lieutenant, Chris Bland. Her Majesty was then shown to her compartment on the train but she first waved the green flag to signal the train out of the station. On the journey the Queen enquired about the countryside, to which the Chairman gave answers about ownership and wildlife matters.

On arrival at Havenstreet the Queen visited the signal box and the Signalman Stuart Duddy explained some of the finer points of our system, then it was off to the Carriage & Wagon Workshop. Director, Brian Bell gave a short address of welcome and Her Majesty then formally opened the workshop by unveiling a plaque and then signing the visitor book. Next it was time for the Queen to meet some of our staff, volunteers and invited guests. After a short time talking to some of the crowd Her Majesty was escorted to the shop where some gifts were presented for the young Royal grandchildren.

All too soon it was time for handshakes and goodbyes, before the Queen was whisked off to the next engagement. It was all too short but it doesn't get better than that. Two visits by the top members of the Royalty really did give the Railway a certain prestige and we were very proud that the powers-that-be felt that the Railway was worthy of this type of official visit. The entire Railway, from the Chairman to the youngest volunteer, can be proud that their achievements over the years have made such visits by Royalty happen. Long may it continue.

Late in 2004, W38 *Ajax* was finally steamed again and the Railway agreed to purchase it from the owner Henry Frampton-Jones for a price that reflected the large amount of work we had put in on the engine. After early steaming, several problems manifested themselves and various visits back to the works had to be made. Never mind, Rome wasn't built in a day and all these snags would be sorted out soon and this handsome looking Barclay will be earning its keep. As a special tribute to the late 'Andy' Anderton, his South African chime whistle now has a permanent home on *Ajax* so there is no longer a fear of marauding elephants on the Isle of Wight Steam Railway!

Top Left: *On a day of particular staff shortage, a visiting VIP was pressed into duty assisting Guard Kim Chalkley; in a role believed not to have been seen before, Her Majesty waves the green flag to the driver of the special train before boarding for the trip to Havenstreet station to open the new Carriage & Wagon Workshop on Wednesday 19th May 2004.* Steve Thearle

Bottom Left: *During a war weekend, a spiv (Steve Castle) tries to entice a land army girl to buy illicit black-market goods, whilst Viv Orchard's Austin truck in the Southern Railway Signal Dept. livery stands outside the signal box at Havenstreet.* Tony Kerley

New Locomotives are Black and Blue All Over!

The final track laying in the Goosefield was completed during the early part of 2005, when a new wheel-drop pit was connected to the sidings. The point needed to put this last piece of trackwork in place was removed from Wootton. For many years a siding had been used there to store an assortment of very elderly stock, and this had been a bit of an eyesore for the local residents. This siding turned off the engine run-round loop and because of the set up of the track, a very sharp curve was needed through this pointwork. This was quite a problem for some of our engines with flanges squealing out their displeasure at having to negotiate such a sharp curve. The decision was made to discontinue the use of the siding and take the point out and move it to the Goosefield at Havenstreet. This would allow us to ease the curve at Wootton and save the cost of the small radius point that would be required for the wheel-drop siding. In November 2004 we removed the point and plain-lined the Wootton loop then, over Christmas and the New Year, we installed the point and connected the wheel-drop siding, commissioning the siding in January 2005.

The restoration of *Calbourne* got the green light early in 2005 with Heritage Lottery funding being granted to partly fund the complete restoration of this unique locomotive. Once the funding had been secured, the work started quickly with the locomotive being stripped to component parts and the boiler being sent to Crewe for major work.

Another WD Austerity tank arrived at the Railway in February 2005 when *Waggoner* came from the then recently-closed Museum of Army Transport at Beverley. It was placed on loan to us by the National Army Museum, the body that owned our other two Army locomotives. After arrival at Havenstreet stripping was started and contractors undertook controlled asbestos removal. Work on the boiler and fitting of air brakes took place and the engine is now in service. We believe that the Railway is now the official custodian of the UK's military strategic steam locomotive reserve!

So that is the story so far, a roller-coaster ride with many ups and a certain amount of downs as well, and forty-years of preservation was the catalyst in writing a book to record the triumphs and disasters and we hope it has done so in an entertaining way. General Manager Hugh Boynton relinquished his post in January 2006 and the Railway welcomed Peter Vail, late of the banking industry, to the position; we understand calculator batteries are still high on the stationery order!

Top Right: *'Andy' Anderton (right) on the footplate of 'Thomas' with fireman Dave Smith in June 2003.* Dave Smith Collection

Middle Right: *Our newest army recruit reports for duty in February 2005, as* Waggoner *transfers to the Havenstreet barracks from Beverley.* Brian Deegan

Bottom Right: *They say everything comes to he who waits, so good reader we can safely say you have waited for most of this book for an action picture of* Ajax *and here it is. As Ajax is finally in steam although a few problems were to slow its progress.* Brian Deegan

Below: *In conclusion we see W8* Freshwater *as it hauls a maximum 100-ton load up the 1:68 gradient out of Havenstreet during the summer of 2005*. IWR Collection

ACKNOWLEDGEMENTS

If you have found enjoyment by reading this volume, we are glad because both authors have invested a large part of their lives in trying to make the Isle of Wight Steam Railway an enjoyable place to visit and something a little special in railway preservation circles. The Isle of Wight Railway is a little different, for we are not trying to be all things to all men, as the Railway has always had an ideal to which it has tried to adhere. The preservationists of the 1960s started with a vision of preserving a small piece of pure Isle of Wight railway history; employing authentic engines pulling equally authentic coaches through the unspoiled countryside of the Garden Isle. Personally we think we have achieved this and many leading people within preservation associations think the same.

It now only remains for us to thank everyone involved with the Isle of Wight Railway in the earliest days way back in the 1960s when the dream began. We must next thank all those who have joined in through the years and have contributed so much, as well as those still involved, either as staff or volunteers. The Ealing Comedy film, *The Titfield*

Thunderbolt of 1952 made railway preservation look very easy, but try telling that to some of our number! Many have been mentioned by name in this book, but far too many have not as we sadly cannot thank everyone personally, nor can we thank all our paying visitors, so this is to you all: well done on 40-years, here's to the next 40, we hope the IW Railway will carry on going from strength to strength!

The authors are indebted to all those who have supplied photographs and their efforts have been individually credited. In addition, we extend very special thanks to Paddy Jardine and Norman Thearle for access to the IW Steam Railway archive and an unpublished manuscript by Ron Strutt. Jeff Layfield and Mike Lambert have given us unfettered access to the *Island Rail News* collection and scanned numerous images. Roger Silsbury has supplied material from the Railway's photo archive. In addition special thanks go to Des Hawkins, Richard Newman, George Wheeler, Iain Whitlam, Jim Loe and Ron Lee for their assistance in ways too numerous to mention. Our very special thanks go to all the members of the Isle of Wight Steam Railway without whom none of this would have been possible! For that reason, all royalties from this publication will pass to the IW Steam Railway.